CITY OF THE UNDEAD

LOUISIANA STATE UNIVERSITY PRESS
BATON ROUGE

CITY of THE UNDEAD

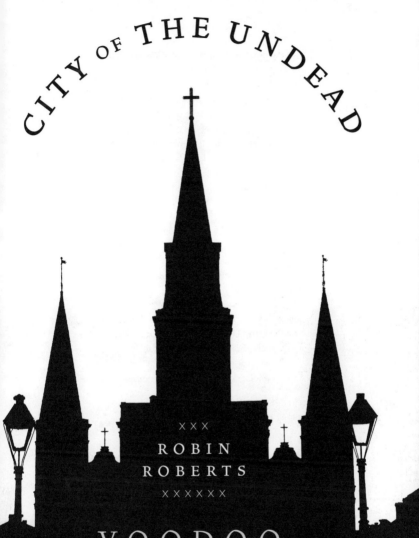

× × ×

ROBIN
ROBERTS

× × × × × ×

VOODOO,
GHOSTS &
VAMPIRES of
NEW ORLEANS

Published with the assistance of the V. Ray Cardozier Fund

Published by Louisiana State University Press
lsupress.org

Manufactured in the United States of America
FIRST PRINTING

LSU Press Paperback Original

DESIGNER: Michelle A. Neustrom
TYPEFACES: Vendetta OT, display; Arno Pro, text
PRINTER AND BINDER: Sheridan Books, Inc.

A portion of chapter 2 was first published as *"Frank's Place,* Gender,
and New Orleans: Using Folklore to Create Televisual Place,"
Journal of Film & Video 69, no. 4 (2017): 28–42.

Cover photograph courtesy 123RF.com/legacy1995.

LIBRARY OF CONGRESS CATALOGING-IN-PUBLICATION DATA

Names: Roberts, Robin, 1957– author.
Title: City of the undead : voodoo, ghosts, and vampires of New Orleans / Robin
    Roberts.
Description: Baton Rouge : Louisiana State University Press, [2023] | "LSU Press
    Paperback Original"—T.p. verso. | Includes bibliographical references and index.
Identifiers: LCCN 2023012374 (print) | LCCN 2023012375 (ebook) |
    ISBN 978-0-8071-8026-6 (paperback) | ISBN 978-0-8071-8111-9 (pdf) |
    ISBN 978-0-8071-8110-2 (epub)
Subjects: LCSH: Death—Louisiana—New Orleans. | Haunted Places—
    Louisiana—New Orleans. | Vodou—Louisiana—New Orleans—History. |
    Vampires—Louisiana—New Orleans. | Ghosts—Louisiana—New Orleans. |
    New Orleans (La.)—Religious life and customs. | New Orleans (La.)—
    Social life and customs.
Classification: LCC GT3211.N4 R6 2023 (print) | LCC GT3211.N4 (ebook) |
    DDC 133.1/290976335—dc23/eng/20230516
LC record available at https://lccn.loc.gov/2023012374
LC ebook record available at https://lccn.loc.gov/2023012375

To my students, who encouraged me
not to be afraid of the supernatural, and to my teachers,
especially Andrea Sununu, John Lemley, William Quillian
(Mount Holyoke College), Nina Auerbach, and William Patrick Day
(University of Pennsylvania), who challenged my assumptions
and inspired me by their teaching and writing.
And of course, this book is dedicated
to Les Wade and New Orleans,
who made it possible.

CONTENTS

x x x

ILLUSTRATIONS

x x x

ACKNOWLEDGMENTS

x x x

This book came into being because Jenny Keegan, acquisitions editor at LSU Press, told me there was a need for a book on New Orleans and the supernatural. Encouraging and supportive, Jenny demonstrates professionalism and acuity, showing that editors are critical to scholarship. May there be more like her.

I also owe a debt to the anonymous reader who read the manuscript carefully and whose suggestions were insightful and constructive. Gail Naron Chalew scrutinized and improved the manuscript's prose. Ashley Gilly astutely identified a critical consistency error and also took the time to locate dialogue errors from a specific episode of a TV show. Catherine Kadair, managing editor at LSU Press, was encouraging and ensured that the manuscript was put into the best possible shape. I am grateful for their professionalism.

My friend and LSU colleague Angeletta Gourdine read many versions of this manuscript; her comments always improved the argument. Members of writing groups at LSU and the University of Arkansas, especially Carolyn Ware, Yajaira Padilla, Lissette Szwdycky-Lopez, Susan Marren, and Kirsten Erikson, offered encouragement through their own examples of scholarly dedication. Frank de Caro and Rosan Jordan first introduced me to Louisiana folklore, and their work has been a guiding light. Finally, my sister Linda Roberts has been a lifelong supporter of my work. I owe more to her than I can say.

Indexers are insufficiently appreciated. Their labors make a book accessible. I am very appreciative of Kristin Kirkpatrick's work in creating the index for this book.

Finally, I wish to thank the *Journal of Film & Video;* a portion of chapter 2 was first published in its pages.

CITY OF THE UNDEAD

THE CITY THAT
DREAMS

× × ×

New Orleans, the city
that dreams stories.
—ANDREI CODRESCU

ndrei Codrescu, a poet who was my colleague for many
years at Louisiana State University, has it right: New Orleans is a city that dreams, as well as a city of dreams. Numerous writers and residents comment on the city's unique culture
and personality, identifying its vibrant street culture, extraordinary
hybrid cuisine, dynamic music scene, compelling visual artists, and
world-renowned festivals. But one of the city's features that is also
well known, though perhaps understandably less examined, is its
connection to the supernatural. Although most people are fascinated and some are repulsed by Voodoo, ghosts, and vampires, the
supernatural remains a subject hard to capture. True believers are
loath to spill their secrets, as Brenda Marie Osbey, a former LSU
colleague and a recent Louisiana state poet laureate, explains in her
essay "Why We Can't Talk to You about Voodoo." Others who had
supernatural experiences may be embarrassed to reveal what they
saw or heard. Yet over the three centuries of the city's existence,
there have been numerous accounts of the paranormal, and these
narratives help define and shape not only the city's sense of itself but
also its appeal to visitors. Live performances such as walking tours
and street theater, as well as films and television series, take place
in the city, and the physical environment—the buildings, the gas-

lights, the fog—reinforces the sense of the supernatural and helps make New Orleans one of the world's top ten tourist destinations.

This book's title, *City of the Undead,* indicates my attention to varieties of the supernatural that focus on the state of being unliving. The "undead" can take different forms. For Voodoo practitioners, a type of death occurs when they give their body over to the possession of a god. Having invited the god into this world through their bodies, the practitioners' physical selves and personalities go into suspension. (Zombies, humans who have died and are reanimated, are a Haitian practice involving drugs and living people and are not part of New Orleans Voodoo.) Ghosts are the manifestation of people who have died, but whose spirits refuse to leave the earth. And vampires once were human but have been converted into potentially immortal blood drinkers. Although vampires walk the earth, they cannot have children, and their bodies are husks kept animated by the infusion of human blood.

One of New Orleans's well-known nicknames, the "Big Easy," refers to the city's tolerance and acceptance of a wide range of cultures and lifestyles. The nickname evokes the city's legalization of prostitution in 1897 in a section known as Storyville; twenty years later, military authorities demanded that prostitution be shut down. However, as this book will show, the city embraces other marginalized beings, such as the undead. Or, as local writer Chris Rose says, "We put the fun in funeral" (12). Following a custom that became popular in the late nineteenth century, many African American funerals in New Orleans have public processions with brass bands, which are known as "second line parades." Mournful, sonorous, slow music—hymns like "Just a Closer Walk with Thee"—is played as the musicians, family, friends, and strangers follow the hearse to the cemetery. But after the body is laid to rest, the music turns upbeat and has a fast beat. Participants wave fans and handkerchiefs to songs like "When the Saints Go Marching In." These public processions keep alive the idea that life and death are inextricable. In the twenty-first century, parades honoring both local and famous people continue in New Orleans, often lasting for hours.

Another compelling New Orleans tradition takes place on Mardi Gras, which otherwise is a festive celebration of the flesh. An African American group, the North Side Skull and Bones Gang, appears early on Mardi Gras Day, walking through downtown New Orleans in handmade skeleton outfits with papier-mâché masks and headpieces, sporting bloody aprons and wielding bones. Calling out "You next!" and "If you don't live right, the Bone Man is coming for ya!" and other threatening phrases, the Skull and Bones Gang admonishes neighborhood children—and adults. This custom reminds all viewers that death lies very close, even on a day of celebration. Historically an African American tradition (though it has expanded to other communities in the city), the Skull and Bones Gang offers a vivid example of the city's unique relationship with the dead.

That celebrated New Orleans Voodoo does not include zombies as a prominent feature illuminates the special role of the supernatural in New Orleans, especially in its connection to African American culture. The North Side Skull and Bones Gang offers reminders of the value of life. Its message is particularly relevant for those whose ancestors experienced enslavement. As Orlando Patterson, Russ Castronovo, and others explain, the experience of enslavement is a form of social death in which a person is alive but is denied personhood. The concept of the zombie, a mindless creature, is antithetical to the city's embrace of the otherworldly because, as this book argues, the supernatural in New Orleans operates primarily as resistance to injustice and oppression. In contrast to the zombie, the supernatural beings that populate New Orleans are active, engaged beings who exist to remind the living of human values and needs.

The second line parade and other rituals in the city that focus on death offer the tourist a cathartic way to engage with mortality. Given that the dominant attitude toward death in the United States is to hide and ignore it, New Orleans's celebrations provide a unique encounter in their embrace of death. The city has many tourist attractions that feature the undead—from walking tours to museums, shops to cafes. Not only do the living enjoy encountering the undead in person through visits to these attractions but also Hollywood has taken note, with numerous supernatural films and television series set and filmed in New Orleans.

As a resident of New Orleans, I have gone on numerous walking tours, attended spiritual rituals, and even, I think, once seen a ghost. After coauthoring a book on New Orleans's Mardi Gras, I decided that I wanted to know more about the Big Easy's other lure—its supernatural history. Much of what is known about that history circulates now through texts that mine and revise the folklore accounts. Fictional texts like movies and television series attest to the authenticity of the supernatural in many ways, reinforced by filming on location in New Orleans.

The stories the city tells about itself and those written by folklorists, novelists, and television and film writers all work to create and sustain a sense of wonder about New Orleans. At the same time, these narratives provide an in-depth engagement with the city's culture. This book examines some of the most influential narratives, identifying their common features. *City of the Undead* also explores what can be verified, through contemporary sources and archives, of the sources of recent paranormal texts set in New Orleans.

That this aspect of the city's culture has long been a mainstay of its tourist appeal is seen by the many walking tours with names like "Haunted History," "French Quarter Vampire Tour," and "New Orleans Drunken Voodoo, Mystery, Paranormal, Supernatural, and History Tour." Yet, few works focus exclusively on the supernatural side of New Orleans in its historical and popular culture context. Books such as *Spirits of New Orleans, The Haunted History of New Orleans,* and *Haunted New Orleans* offer only brief sketches of reported supernatural events and characters; their encyclopedic approach does not consider why the three major supernatural categories—Voodoo practitioners, ghosts, and vampires—are so prevalent in the city. How did New Orleans come to be known as America's most haunted city? Why do so many writers set their supernatural tales in the Big Easy? Why do locals embrace this version of New Orleans—with some moving to the city because of its supernatural appeal?

After an introductory chapter, *City of the Undead* examines the sometimes contradictory accounts of the Voodoo queen (the term used here is one of respect and authority, as it is used by Queen Latifah and other Black artists), the ghost, and the vampire. Rooted in New Orleans's unique mixture of Native American, European, African, and Caribbean cultures, these figures mutated in the New World. Adhering to source cultures and providing a means of adapting to harsh and brutal physical conditions and legal oppressions, they offer solace and alternatives to the injustice experienced by so many in what became the United States. Beliefs in these figures and competing versions of their stories illustrate the conflict and struggle for power and authority of the city's many heritages. Even though the supernatural is, by definition, otherworldly, its creatures emerge out of actual history, out of people's struggles and conflicts and terrible injustices such as enslavement. As the city grew on the backs and from the blood of Native and African Americans, so the supernatural came to reflect and even focus on their traumatic and exploitative experiences.

Writers such as the previously mentioned Orlando Patterson and Russ Castronovo, as well as Tiya Miles, have helped chart the meaning of the supernatural for enslaved peoples and their descendants. Patterson traces the practice to antiquity and describes its meaning and purpose in later societies. A sociologist, he introduced the concept of "social death" for the enslaved and the institution of slavery: enslaved people were both people and property, and this irreconcilable conflict caused white supremacist society to engage in social and psychological contortions to enable it to rationalize its brutal exploitation. As a people already denied full human existence, the enslaved point to the boundary between life and death, and so their stories engage the supernatural directly. Castronovo (2001) examines political states' need to have their citizens be quiescent, "necro citizens" and demonstrates how the enslaved and women offer examples of social death, exclusion, and domination by white men through political discourse. And Tiya Miles analyzes ghost tours and narratives in Savannah, Charleston, and New Orleans to see whether the appropriation of African American history is presented "in a way that outweighs the value of inclusion" (123). Although Miles finds their reiteration of racist stereotypes too overt to justify the way the tours present African American history, she does assert the importance of place to these stories. In examining one place, New Orleans, and its depiction of a range of supernatural figures, I too find both troubling and encouraging elements. By focusing on the supernatural narrative, New Orleans tells pieces of its history that are elsewhere minimized. And the supernatural also claims a central place in the city's identity. New Orleans as a supernatural place has an impact not only on tourists but also on a worldwide audience: the readers of novels and the viewers of television shows and films.

City of the Undead offers a unique overview of the city's supernatural side, beginning with its historical roots. Chapter 1, "A Crypt of the Supernatural," surveys the city's history of catastrophe from its Native American beginnings to the twenty-first century, focusing on how these major events helped define the city's focus on death. In addition to presenting major events and how New Orleanians coped with death in their midst, this chapter addresses the unique convergence of culture and attitudes toward the afterlife. The mix of cultures, combined with the city's geography and climate, created a perfect place for belief in the undead.

Chapter 2, "Feminine Power and New Orleans's Voodoo Queen," addresses the life of the famous Marie Laveau. An actual woman—or women, depending on which account you believe—Marie Laveau exerted power in a city at a time when slavery was still legal. A rich mixture of African and Haitian spiritual practices came to New Orleans with the people who were abducted and brought here as slaves; those who were born here and those who came here after the revolution in the French colony of St. Domingue in 1809 continued their ancestors' practices. The post-revolution immigration from what is now Haiti doubled the city's population in a matter of months, and the new residents had a profound impact on New Orleans.

Voodoo shops for tourists and locals still flourish in New Orleans. The appeal of Voodoo as an alternative to traditional justice and medical practice continues. Marie Laveau's life remains shrouded in mystery, but like the figure of the vampire, she has a powerful existence in literature. Drawing on the two major biographies of Laveau, this chapter explores a television depiction of Voodoo in the critically acclaimed 1980s series *Frank's Place*, Jewell Parker Rhodes's 1993 novel *Voodoo Dreams*, and *American Horror Story: Coven* (2013–2014), the award-winning television show that features Marie Laveau. Her stature as a powerful figure reinforces both the femininity of Voodoo and New Orleans's identity as a city that provides alternatives to the U.S. narrative of individual white male achievement. Although there are male figures associated with Voodoo, particularly versions of Dr. John/Papa Legba, in recent popular culture representations—*Voodoo Dreams, American Horror Story: Coven,* and even the Disney animated film *The Princess and the Frog*—Laveau not only exemplifies the undead in turning her body over to Voodoo deities to achieve her goals but also defines Voodoo as a presence in the city, a hundred and fifty years after her death.

Chapter 3, "America's Most Haunted City," addresses the city's well-deserved reputation. Real estate signs even advertise property, especially homes in the French Quarter, as "haunted" or "not haunted." Restaurants such as Muriel's, located near the St. Louis Cathedral, keep one table open, even at the busiest times, for their ghosts. This chapter discusses LSU Press's republication of Jeanne deLavigne's 1946 *Ghost Stories of Old New Orleans,* the 2013–2014 season of *American Horror Story: Coven,* and Victoria Schwab's 2021 novel, *Bridge of Souls.* As Jeffrey Weinstock explains, ghosts function "as a form of cultural critique" (2), and New Orleans's many ghosts expose racism and sexism in both the city's past and present. Unsurprisingly, many of the city's ghosts emerge from the presence of pirates, the torments endured by the enslaved, and the mistreatment of women by their lovers, husbands, fathers, and even grandfathers. In keeping with New Orleans's character as a feminine city, female ghosts in particular refuse to remain silent in death, though they lacked opportunities to defend themselves when living. And the humans who see ghosts often are women, reinforcing the gendering of this supernatural figure. While Voodoo priestesses can call on deities and use herbs to create potions, ghosts are liminal, shadowy, and often ignored by the living. Even when male, ghosts are thus feminized and subordinate, living in the shadows. The popular television show *Ghost Hunters* reveals a contemporary way to uncover ghosts through technology. In multiple visits to New Orleans, paranormal investigators help define New Orleans's spirits and engage them by being sympathetic to the mistreatment they suffered as living beings.

Chapter 4, "Drinking Blood in the Big Easy," focuses on the blood-sucking species first popularized in the film *Nosferatu* and Bram Stoker's *Dracula*. European in origin, the vampire flourishes in New Orleans's imagination. The city's historic French Quarter and Garden District contain many beautiful old homes and streets that, gas lit and surrounded by mature oak trees and Spanish moss, evoke mystery—and centuries of exploitation. The city's infamous reputation as a major site of markets for the enslaved contributes to a mystical, supernatural exploitation of the living by the undead. Although there are a few gory tales of vampires in New Orleans's history, the city's claim to be a "vampire city" really took hold after Anne Rice's 1976 novel, *Interview with the Vampire*. Performed by fans and professionals, characters from her novels such as Lestat appear at masquerade balls, vampire film festivals, walking tours, the Boutique du Vampyre, and Vampire Café, offering a "vampire experience" for visitors and locals. New Orleans even has the distinction of being a major home for "vampire lifestylers," people who meet and socialize, engaging in a range of simulated and even actual blood-imbibing practices.

Adaptations of *Interview with the Vampire* as a 1994 film and a 2022 television series help keep Rice's unique and slightly more flattering vision of vampires alive. Her main character Louis is a somewhat reluctant vampire who appreciates beauty and who relishes the aesthetics and energy of his hometown of New Orleans. A 2013–2018 television series, *The Originals,* also set in New Orleans, even gives credit to vampires for establishing and running New Orleans for hundreds of years. George R. R. Martin, author of the *Game of Thrones* series, created a sympathetic vampire in his 1982 novel *Fevre Dream,* which develops the link between vampirism and slavery. And *Dracula 2000,* a film, that like these other texts emphasizes the parallels between New Orleans and vampires, evokes the city's Catholic heritage and the contrast between its religiosity and its hedonism.

All vampire texts draw on the city's geography, architecture, and culture to suggest that its decay makes it a suitable home for the undead. Where Voodoo and ghosts offer a feminine alternative to capitalism and technology (more about this tension later in the book), vampires present an alternative to traditional masculinity. The shadowy existence of vampires and their association with a feudal order underscore New Orleans as a city that progress and industry have passed by.

Although this book examines the major figures of Voodoo priestess, ghost, and vampire in separate chapters, visitors and citizens of New Orleans can encounter and accept the reality of all these supernatural creatures. As the stories about otherworldly beings often reveal, supernatural creatures can have very human conflicts about territory. Humans can become caught up in these struggles and then advocate for one type of creature over the other. Some living beings choose to believe that one group—say ghosts—is "real" but vampires don't exist. Yet, because Voodoo practitioners, ghosts, and vampires (and their fans) all lay claim to the city, New Orleans finds itself to be desirable supernatural real estate.

It is hard to overstate the cathartic importance of the supernatural for residents and visitors to the city. New Orleans's history explains its fascination with death and its reputation as a supernatural city. By journeying to New Orleans, we can experience the thrills and emotions associated with death, but with the reassurance of the supernatural that there is life after death and that resistance to injustice does not end in the grave.

This book's focus on New Orleans's history and its link to the supernatural, as well as on the city's many tales of spirits that are performed on the streets (in walking tours), in fiction, and on television and film screens, will illuminate how these various formats work to reinforce the city's identity as the city of the undead. If you have taken a walking tour, you will perhaps be surprised to find many of the stories you hear can be traced to local folk tales. If you read novels, you will notice how fiction and literary devices appear on walking tours and how they draw tourists to the city. If you are a devotee of the many paranormal television shows and films set in the city, you will discover how contemporary media rely heavily on history. Perhaps most importantly, *City of the Undead* presents a case for seeing the place itself as essential to the many human-created narratives of the supernatural. Voodoo queens, ghosts, and even vampires, after all, exist primarily for human consumption and human entertainment. To walk the streets of New Orleans offers a rare opportunity for a visitor to experience what it could feel like to experience the paranormal, to experience a frisson of fear, but one that can be safely contained and turned into a story when you return home. If, even briefly, this book helps you understand a New Orleans experience—whether it is live or through a story—*City of the Undead* will have achieved its purpose.

1

A CRYPT OF
THE SUPERNATURAL

X X X

In New Orleans, where dreams
are spoken in the streets at more frequent
intervals than anywhere else in North America,
otherwise intangible possibilities become
all the more sensuously visible,
audible, and touchable.

—JOSEPH ROACH

On a cold December night, I was on a ghost tour with friends and family who were visiting New Orleans. While the tour guide was a compelling speaker, our attention would drift away as we tried to keep warm. The weather, however, was perfect for a ghost tour—we were already shivering. When we arrived in front of a Decatur Street mansion, a wispy mist began hovering over the rooftops, an effect of the nearby Mississippi River and the cold. But as the tour guide began to tell the story of Julie, a woman of color who braved a night on that very roof to secure her white male partner's promise of marriage, the mist seemed to take on human form. A few in the group gasped, including me. As her story was recounted, some of us began to see a female shape up on the roof, just for a moment. The tour guide was not surprised by our reaction, only nodding her head as she continued the tragic tale of the woman's death. Feeling a paranormal presence, if only for seconds, changes how you view what many dismiss as an illusion. Many writers and tour guides spice their accounts of the paranormal in New Orleans with personal experiences, and these firsthand encounters with the supernatural draw many visitors to the city. The city's history and its various cultures that mingled for hundreds of years corroborate the presence of the supernatural.

This chapter focuses on the culture and geography of New Orleans to explore why it is one of the most famous paranormal sites. The city is a character in supernatural tales as powerful and important as the figures discussed in the rest of this book. In addition to its unique geography, the city's various groups hold overlapping spiritual beliefs that, to give an oft-used metaphor, create a gumbo—a rich and potent stew of the paranormal. Understanding the ways that Native American, African American, and European (especially Catholic) customs address life after death illuminates the city's stories about the undead. Providing an overview of the supernatural and its key figures—the Voodoo queen, the ghost, and the vampire—in New Orleans, this chapter prepares you for the more specific analyses in subsequent chapters. Before we meet Marie Laveau, the Voodoo queen, and the numerous ghosts and vampires of New Orleans, it helps to know more about the city.

While we conventionally think of cities as physical sites, Steve Pile (1, 3) points out in *Real Cities: Modernity, Space, and the Phantasmagorias of City Life* that a city is more than that: it is "a state of mind" and is "as much emotional as physical, as much visible as invisible." Cities are not mere accretions of physical space and buildings but exist as imagined and sustained by people, practices, and beliefs. Although any city founded hundreds of years ago may claim supernatural inhabitants and uncanny events, New Orleans's unique history has specific features that produce its many historical and fictitious tales of horror. The city's verifiable history has led to its "haunted history." At the same time, it is a "city haunted by its misdeeds," as Pile describes London (8).

In *Unfathomable City: A New Orleans Atlas,* Rebecca Solnit and Rebecca Snedeker describe the city as having a particular association with the dead: "New Orleans has an undying past . . . the old sins and rites are still alive here; . . . the dead never go away but remain as an ancestral population. You could say that death lives here" (11). New Orleans's cemeteries "are cities of the dead where the living visit . . . where descendants decorate the graves of their relations and picnic with them." Just as in southern Louisiana's landscape there are sometimes unclear boundaries between land and water, the region's first peoples understood life and death to be intertwined, closer to the beliefs of some African religious cultures than to the separation of life from death held by the European colonists. Solnit and Snedeker suggest that New Orleans's geographic fluidity explains why it is a city "where the boundaries between life and death are thin, in the most spiritual and brutal ways" (34).

While never officially sanctioned by European colonists, the views of Native Americans and African Americans about the permeability of the boundaries between life and death held a sway and fascination on all who lived in New Orleans. Significantly, the depiction of vampires, ghosts, and Voodoo priestesses in New Orleans reflects how "belief in ancestors also testifies to the inclusive nature of traditional African spirituality by positing that deceased progenitors still play a role in the lives of their living descendants." In describing these practices, Jacob Olupona notes that "followers can seek spiritual direction and relief from healers, medicine men and women, charms [adornments often worn to bring good luck], amulets [adornments often used to ward off evil], and diviners [spiritual advisers]" (Chiorazzi).

That in New Orleans Native Americans and Africans held similar worldviews and beliefs and were able to maintain their ancestral spiritual practices, despite oppression and legal prohibition of their rituals, are key factors in producing the city's supernatural aura. From its earliest days as a colonized place, New Orleans contained large groups of people who resisted a more restrictive view of the relationships between living and dead people, between humanity and the natural world, and the role of women in that world.

New Orleans has long been celebrated as a site of supernatural happenings, and its infamous "cities of the dead"—its above-ground cemeteries—are on a lengthy list of historical features that justify the city's claim as "America's most haunted city." To be a city of the undead, it is first necessary to have legions of people who die. From its importance as a site of Native American spirituality and commerce to its struggles with deadly yellow fever and malaria epidemics, from its being a major site of buying and selling of humans into slavery to its adaptations of Haitian Vodou and African Vodun, the city's diverse mixture of cultures has produced its reputation as a home for the undead.

Native Americans have lived in South Louisiana for millennia, as attested by the ancient mounds still in existence in the state. Six tribes of Native Americans lived in Louisiana at the time of European contact (see figure 1), including the Attakapa, whose name means "human flesh eater" (Wall 5). The Chitimacha, who inhabited an area south of New Orleans, were a large tribe with a well-developed religious structure (7). In the early 1700s, the colony established by the French was struggling, and it was only with the aid of Native Americans that the colonists were able to survive. Rev. D. L. "Goat" Carson, a Cherokee medicine man and musician, notes that the place where New Orleans was founded was for centuries a Native American ceremonial area: "It was called the city of the ancient ones. They had a temple city here. They had a holy city here" (Osborn). Citing the presence of the Choctaw, Natchez, Muskogee, and Creek tribes, Carson explains, "There has always been a blending of red and black going on since the very beginning. [Native Americans and African Americans] had cultural similarities. They understood the universe in a mystical way, in a spiritual way" (Osborn).

Mostly written out of New Orleans history, Native American tribes and their contributions to the city's supernatural status deserve more acknowledgment and research. In the eighteenth century, "an anonymous French source . . . talked about [Native American] relatives killed in war as 'ghosts' who 'have not been given certain effects on dying of which they had need in the other world.'

FIG. 1. *Taking Possession of Louisiana and the River Mississippi . . .*
by Cavelier de la Salle . . . 9th of April 1682, by Jean Adolph Bocquin, ca. 1860.
Courtesy of the Historic New Orleans Collection, Acc. no. 1970.1.

Ghosts needed to be quieted by vengeance and proper ceremony"
(Garrison and O'Brien 72).

The presence of Native American figures in New Orleans Black
Spiritual churches also attests to the continuing influence of Native
American concepts. As Claude Francis Jacobs and Andrew Kaslow
(1991) explain, "The New Orleans Spiritual churches constitute a
distinctive African American belief system. Influenced by Catholicism, Pentecostalism, Spiritualism, and Voodoo, the group is a New
World syncretic faith, similar to Espiritismo, Santería, and Um-
banda." Reflecting their alternative worldview to traditional male-
dominated Christianity, these churches were founded by women.
In their worship, "stereotypical representations of Native Americans become icons of spiritual power, inspiring a wide range of be-

liefs and behaviors in non-Natives" (Wehmeyer 16). In a detailed analysis of Native American figures in New Orleans's Spiritual churches, Wehmeyer concludes, "They remain among the most celebrated and venerated figures" (21), and there are "a number of similarities to several important figures in the pantheons of related African and Afro-Caribbean religions" (23). Even though Native American groups in the New Orleans area were in some cases exterminated and in other instances relocated and their land stolen, they were able to intermingle with enslaved African Americans and support them in their quest for freedom.

Enslaved Africans, mostly from the Senegambia region in West Africa, arrived in the city several years after New Orleans was founded in 1718. Their shared beliefs and experiences had a great impact not only on the city's survival but also on its culture (see figure 2). Many of those who were enslaved and dragged to Louisiana were members of the Bambara people (Midlo Hall); other Africans were from the Diola, Mande, Mandinga, and Wolof tribes. Even though they came from various tribes, these groups had already incorporated similar items such as gris-gris or charms into their religious practices (Clark 136). Donna Moody notes, "The African Diaspora, whether of voluntary migrations within Africa or forced migrations throughout the Americas by means of the trans-Atlantic slave trade, inevitably produced conditions of cultural and spiritual sharing" among various African cultures (5). Because a large proportion of the enslaved population had a shared cosmology and spiritual beliefs, Africans in Louisiana were able to retain more of their culture than those who were enslaved in other parts of the United States (Midlo Hall 28–55, 96–118). During the years of what is now called the Haitian Revolution, from 1791 to 1804, thousands of opponents of the successful rebellion and their enslaved, most with an African Yoruban heritage, came to New Orleans, increasing the diffusion of similar spiritual beliefs throughout the city. The Creoles, whose higher status as free people of color separated them legally and socially from the enslaved, added another layer of complexity in cultural and spiritual prac-

FIG. 2. *The Bamboula,* by Edward Kemble, drawing made in the late
nineteenth century. Courtesy of the Historic New Orleans
Collection, Acc. no. 1974.25.10.54.

tice. And because "African American and people of mixed race
comprised a majority of the city's population" (Dedek 120) by 1810,
these shared beliefs played a major role in shaping New Orleans's
culture.

A short description of African spiritual beliefs cannot do justice to their depth, complexity, and richness; for the purposes of
exploring the dominance of the supernatural in New Orleans, the
most relevant feature is the African worldview, shared by local Native Americans, of a holistic universe, one in which the living and
the dead are not separate. Olupona, for example, explains, "African
spirituality simply acknowledges that beliefs and practices touch
on and inform every facet of human life, and therefore African religions cannot be separated from the everyday or mundane. African
spirituality is truly holistic" (Chiorazzi). In contrast to Europeans,
Native Americans, African Americans, and Creoles (free people of color who were predominantly Catholic) saw the natural
and supernatural as closely connected and equally powerful. As

Christine Leigh Heyrman (2000) notes of Native Americans, people of color "perceived the 'material' and 'spiritual' as a unified realm of being—a kind of extended kinship network. . . . By contrast, Protestant and Catholic traditions were more inclined to emphasize the gulf that separated the pure, spiritual beings in heaven—God, the angels, and saints—from sinful men and women mired in a profane world filled with temptation and evil."

Moody documents that "Native American and African American material culture of mid-19th century to [the] present day appear to hold evidence for a more ancient spiritual and cultural relationship between these two diverse peoples. There is evidence of strikingly similar, and in some instances, identical, pre-Columbian (before 1492) symbols from Africa and North America" (v). In her analysis of symbols that appear in both Native American and African American material culture, including quilts, she finds that many "used in contemporary work by American Indians and African Americans are connected to ancient oral traditions of cosmology and creation" (11), particularly the African cosmogram: "This image depicts the ancient African belief system of birth, life, death, and rebirth, and the world of the living and that of the spirit world, or world of the dead. The world of the living and the spirit world are separated by water" (27). With the Mississippi River, which local Native American tribes called the "Father of Rivers," and its swampland, New Orleans offered a setting befitting this worldview. "In the Indigenous worldview, our physical and spiritual lives must be in balance with all of the natural world around us as well as all that is contained in the universe" (67). This worldview led to a much greater appreciation for and acceptance of the supernatural, especially the ideas that the dead and the living are connected, that the living should communicate with the dead, and that the dead can aid the living.

Although traditional Christian teaching acknowledges that Jesus rose from the dead, his resurrection is depicted as unique to his godliness. In contrast, Native American and African American religions could accept and even attempt to enact the reanimation of the dead or at least communicate with and receive assistance from elders who had died. Native American and African American veneration for ancestors enabled them to be part of everyday life. West African beliefs allowed for the possession of a living being by a godlike being, and for many tribes, artifacts could be imbued with power. The idea of curses and cursed objects, as well as protective charms, was a material aspect of these belief systems. The natural world, both animals and plants, was venerated and respected, rather than being seen as a setting to be dominated and exploited by humans. Women held greater power in Indigenous and African American beliefs than they do in Catholicism, where Mary, the mother of Christ, was an intercessor rather than a figure with power in her own right. The Native American and African American spiritual figures upheld a compelling and attractive religious practice.

Catholicism was more amenable than Protestantism to contacting the dead and even made room for accommodating believers in Voodoo. Some Catholic practices, such as praying to the saints, were part of Voodoo believers' practices, and the use of reliquaries and other material objects in folk practices resembles aspects of Voodoo. That New Orleans was for so many years ruled by Catholic colonial powers—first the French, then the Spanish, and then the French again before the Louisiana Purchase in 1803—made it more open to African and Indigenous worldviews. As Midlo Hall explains, "Like the Indians and the Africans, the Europeans were acculturated by the people, and by the world they encountered" in what became Louisiana (xiv). She also reminds readers of the early Europeans' dependence on the Indigenous people, noting that "early Louisiana settlements began as Indian villages" and that French soldiers were sent to those villages to avoid starvation (15). French fur traders and Jesuit priests often lived with the Native Americans, enabling a mingling of spiritual beliefs. Thus, Catholicism in the New World was closer to Indigenous peoples' spirituality than Protestantism, and it is due in part, as Midlo Hall notes, to "the Anglophone orientation of American historians" (xv) that

New Orleans appears as a strange place with strange beliefs that, from a Protestant perspective, seemed very exotic.

Christian, Native American, and African American Creole Catholic beliefs were sometimes held and practiced at the same time. Clark describes the complex mixture of peoples during the colonial period of the city as stoking "a creolization process fueled by unsteady white control, the close relationship between white and Native families, and a reliance on enslaved African labor" (134). Yet, even though Native American and African American beliefs about life and death surely offered solace and escape from the brutal realities of European exploitation and abuse, their adherents were not free to practice those religions. The power and threat posed by Native American and African American beliefs to European control meant that these practices were outlawed and suppressed, even as some Europeans and free people of color consulted Voodoo practitioners and participated in Voodoo rituals.

As mentioned, Catholicism, rather than the more literalist and ascetic Protestantism, was the religion of the first European colonists, which made for a fertile combination with Native American and African cultural practices, culminating in Carnival parades and costumes that flourished in the city. Catholicism and Voodoo, strengthened by an influx of thousands of Haitian refugees in 1809, existed side by side (https://www.wwno.org/podcast /tripod-new-orleans-at-300/2017-10-27/haiti-new-orleans-is-the -feeling-mutual). Both whites and Blacks reportedly consulted the noted Voodoo priestess Marie Laveau during her long life in nineteenth-century New Orleans. Laveau was baptized and married in St. Louis Cathedral (see figure 3), and her above-ground grave in St. Louis Cemetery #1 is still a pilgrimage site for people hoping for her intercession (see figure 4). The overlap and contiguity of both Catholicism and Voodoo continue today, as noted by Dianne Honoré, a noted culture bearer of the city: "While I attended the St. Louis Cathedral Academy as a young girl, I met a Voodoo practitioner at the back gates of my school. The woman gave me a blessing that included bones and pennies" (quoted in

FIG. 3. Jackson Square, or the Place des Armes, with St. Louis Cathedral
at the center. Gift of Mr. Boyd Cruise. Courtesy of the Historic
New Orleans Collection, Acc. no. 1974.25.23.54.

Roberts 50). Another New Orleans resident, Karen Jeffries, was
drawn to the city in the 1990s, in part by Anne Rice's novel, *Interview with the Vampire*; Jeffries soon encountered ghosts and became a paranormal researcher. After attending a public Voodoo
ceremony for protection against hurricanes, led by Priestess Sallie
Ann Glassman, Jeffries became fascinated with this religion, eventually becoming an initiated Voodoo priestess herself. Voodoo,
Jeffries explains, is a religion of light and love, and any gris-gris
she creates focuses on opening a person's heart. Before she became a priestess, however, Jeffries benefited from cleansing rituals
to restore and protect her from an evil ghost. Jeffries also leads a
powerful prayer group that draws on her Christian upbringing and
whose practices are indistinguishable from Catholicism's call for
blessing and succor for the ill. In this way, contemporary Voodoo
practitioners continue the mingling or overlay of Catholicism and
Voodoo that was inevitable in a colony in which Catholicism was
the state religion.

The convergence of Native American, African, and European
spiritual beliefs is evident in All Saints' Day celebrations that have
been held in New Orleans cemeteries for nearly three centuries.
Dedek explains, "During the nineteenth century and beyond, peo-

FIG. 4. Sexton or guide at Marie Laveau's tomb.
Courtesy of the Historic New Orleans Collection, Acc. no. 1974.25.23.132.

ple socialized, celebrated, collected alms, married, and cast spells in the cemeteries of New Orleans. All Saints' Day drew on European Catholic practices, but they contained other elements, including lighting up the night with fire" (114–115). For a time, it was not only a religious but also a legal holiday, marked by the closing of government offices, banks, and schools. Its celebratory events were covered extensively in the local newspapers from the early 1800s. The extent of the day's festivities even made it comparable to Mardi Gras: "Like Mardi Gras, All Saints' Day brought the entire city together, functioning not only as a day of communion between the living and the dead, but also the living and the living" (118). Families would socialize in the cemeteries among the graves, eating and drinking. This positive engagement and celebration in cemeteries, was, however, connected with a troubling history of racism.

Code Noir, the French legal system that governed slavery practices, dictated that the enslaved family unit was to be kept together until children were considered adults and that, on holy days and Sundays, the enslaved were allowed to sell their labor or meet in groups; nevertheless, the enslaved remained oppressed, with few legal protections from violent abuse. Sometimes lauded as being "exceptional" for its French Code Noir laws that offered those few meager protections for the enslaved, New Orleans was also a major slave market that produced innumerable horrors for those held in bondage. The terrible legacy of enslavement is reflected in horrific, documented events that are still recounted on walking tours, such as the actions of the evil torturer Madame LaLaurie and the appearances of ghosts unable to rest after death because of their mistreatment as enslaved Africans or freed people of color.

Even after the importation of slaves from outside the United States was legally banned in 1808 (the practice continued illegally for decades afterward), New Orleans continued as a site for trading and selling enslaved people from other parts of the country; the city was known for its brutality. And of course, the Code Noir did not remain the law once the city became Spanish and then American territory in 1803. The city did, however, contain the continent's largest population of freed people of color, which allowed elements of European, African, and Native American cultures to mingle in a more pronounced fashion than elsewhere in the United States. This mingling of cultures produced a more fluid view of life and death than in other U.S. cities and enriched burial customs.

Factors, such as the shortage of women and the practice of plaçage—a socially sanctioned system in which free women of color entered into a marriage-like contract with white men—resulted in New Orleans having the largest population of "Free People of Color" (as designated in the U.S. Census; also known as Creoles). According to the 1860 census, there were 11,000 free people of color in the city, compared to only 335 in the entire state of Texas, only 753 in neighboring Mississippi, and a mere 76 in Arkansas (Dedek 66). Under Reconstruction, which was enforced by federal troops, people of color flourished in educational and political arenas; the first Black governor of Louisiana was elected then. No longer denied the dignity of burials, the formerly enslaved and their children created burial societies and added African elements to their funeral rites. "Following deeply rooted African tradition, the black benevolent [and burial] societies usually involved more ritual, symbolism and religion, and they had a greater economic function" (100) than those founded by European Americans. Yet the aftereffects of being brutally treated during enslavement led to much higher death rates among African Americans than other ethnic groups from 1864 to 1880: 32–82 per 1,000 African Americans versus 5–32 per 1,000 whites (101). As many as 90 percent of Indigenous people are believed to have died from smallpox, and many tribes were completely extinguished by contact with European invaders.

Yet people of all races suffered the miserable and often deadly environment of the city. As Wall and coauthors explain, New Orleans was unhealthier than other cities in the state and elsewhere, in part because of a lack of access to clean water. They describe it as "surely one of America's filthiest and most disease-ridden large cities" (273). Mosquitos carried yellow fever, dengue fever, and malaria, resulting in large numbers of deaths. The rich would flee the city when mosquitos were at their worst in the summer, but everyone was affected to some degree by hookworm, pellagra, rickets, scurvy, and other serious ailments. Historian C. E. Richard describes the dire situation of the city from its onset: "The only thing New Orleans needed more than a hospital, it seemed, was a new cemetery. Smallpox, yellow fever, cholera, scarlet fever, typhoid, and malaria all haunted the port, and disease claimed a share of the population every summer" (20). While the rich were buried in above-ground tombs, the poor and the enslaved were buried in the earth. The latter's graves remain unmarked all over the city (Eaton, "The Lost Graves"). As Richard concludes, "Life in Louisiana was often harsh. And short" (20).

The brutality and brevity of life in eighteenth- and nineteenth-century New Orleans contributed to its unusual custom of above-ground burials in small buildings, set in rows, with alleys between them like streets, complete with street signs (see figure 5). As the city grew more prosperous, tombs became more elaborate. The unusual appearance of these tombs led to these cemeteries being called "cities of the dead." The phrase was used by many early visitors to New Orleans, including architect Benjamin Latrobe in 1819; Rev. Timothy Flint, a tourist from Massachusetts in 1826; and author C. W. Kenworthy. It was mentioned in the New Orleans newspaper, the *Daily Picayune,* in 1838. Popular accounts explained that people were not buried in the ground because of the city's high water table and described the regular occurrence of coffins and bodies popping out of the earth, yet the historical reality was more prosaic. The practice of above-ground burial was common in France and Spain, where many of the colonists originated. But where French and Spanish above-ground interments placed the body in a vault dug on the floor of the tomb, New Orleans corpses were placed inside the tomb walls, usually on a shelf that would be cleared after a year and a day, after the city's intense heat had ensured rapid decomposition of the body.

Even though other cities in the nineteenth century experi-

FIG. 5. St. Louis #1 Cemetery in New Orleans.
Photograph by the author.

enced epidemics, their severity and high mortality rate in New Orleans, along with its unusual above-ground burials in cities of the dead, operated together to encourage the aura of the supernatural. Ornate tombs that resembled small houses offered a physical site that, combined with Native American and African American beliefs about ancestors, made the dead seem akin to the living. This sense of closeness was emphasized by New Orleanians visiting and eating and drinking in cemeteries on All Saints' Day. Made of local brick, New Orleans's tombs required maintenance, and on every November 1, citizens would not only whitewash and repair tombs but also would listen to speeches made by local religious figures and politicians.

Tourists have visited New Orleans and marveled at its funerary customs since the early nineteenth century. As Dedek explains, "The cemeteries came to be among the city's most-visited attractions" (58). That so many cemeteries are within the city limits, in contrast to other major U.S. cities, makes the city's love affair with death and the afterlife inescapable. Dedek notes, "From their humble beginnings, New Orleans's cemeteries evolved along with the city. New Orleans's extreme dedication to commemorating its dead resulted in the cost of burial being higher in New Orleans than in most other cities" (1, 96).

Many of the above-ground tombs are beautifully ornate, adorned with statuary and cemetery art; images of hands and urns and angels often appear. Yet the contrast between the exteriors of the tombs and what happened inside them reflects the beauty and decay that characterize New Orleans. Joe Kissell (2021) describes the process of decomposition of the bodies in the tombs: "Just as an oven would not be constructed to bake a single loaf, the tombs in New Orleans cemeteries are used again and again . . . A typical scenario is that after a year, the bones of the departed are swept into an opening in the floor of a tomb." Cities of the dead make it all too easy to imagine a ghost or a vampire emerging from their small home and mingling with the living. As Kissell notes, "Whereas death is usually kept hidden, buried out of sight, New Orleans gives residents and visitors constant reminders of the impermanence of life."

In a long section on burial societies in his book, Dedek notes their unusual qualities in New Orleans, where the groups not only ensure burial for those who could not afford it but also host parades and festivals: "Pageantry has long been a significant aspect of the culture of New Orleans, and the [burial] societies held elaborate ceremonies." New Orleanians of all racial and economic groups evoke ancient Roman views of the tomb as "a point of contact between the living and the dead" (22).

Macabre stories of corpses buried in watery soil inhabited by crawfish that presumably ate human flesh added to the strange and spooky nature of New Orleans's burials. That these crawfish then were harvested and sold to New Orleanians to eat, often just outside the cemetery gates, adds another layer to the intermingling of water and land in the city's landscape. The illustrious architect Benjamin Latrobe in 1819 recorded this awful account told to him by a traveler to the city: "'Sixty to eighty persons were buried each day, and nothing was to be seen but coffins carried about on all sides . . . Whole streets . . . were cleared by their inhabitants, and New Orleans was literally one vast cemetery" (Sealsfield qtd in Stanonis 249). At this time, New Orleans was the "city with the highest mortality rate in the United States" (251). The extensive cemeteries, their placement within the city, and the celebratory rituals of All Saints' Day and jazz funerals all kept the dead within sight of the living. In addition, the cemeteries were significant sites of material—both physical and emotional—for stories about the undead.

The cemeteries proved fertile ground not only for stories about Voodoo practices but also their actual performance. Voodoo is the most distinctive element of the city of the undead's supernatural aura. Although Voodoo practitioners live in other cities, they have always been more prominent in New Orleans, in part because it is often seen as "the Caribbean's northernmost city." The rapid influx of as many as ten thousand refugees from the Haitian Revolution (75 percent of whom had some African ancestors) in the late eighteenth and early nineteenth century rapidly increased not only the city's size but also the influence of Voodoo practices. As Dedek notes, Voodoo believers found a receptive site in New Orleans where "some aspects of West African religion [similar to Voodoo] were already being practiced" (120). Voodoo, "an amalgamation of the traditional religious beliefs of the Ewe, Yoruba, and Fon cultures of West Africa combined with the Catholic faith" (120), is still practiced in the city, but because of its historical repression and the secrecy on the part of its believers, it is difficult to document. What is indisputable is its effect on New Orleans and its supernatural reputation.

In the years before the Louisiana Purchase made New Orleans a part of the United States, Voodoo operated as a form of resistance to the Catholicism legally mandated by the French and Spanish, with enslaved and free people of color "incorporating Catholic imagery and mythology into their existing belief systems" (Dedek 120). New Orleans Voodoo differs from that practiced in Haiti or in African countries, in that there are fewer deities and Catholic saints are part of the pantheon; it also lacks the focus on "Li Grande Zombi" and on summoning spirits of the dead. An important feature of New Orleans Voodoo is calling on the gods, including Damballah, the rainbow serpent and prime deity, and Papa Legba, who acts as a gateway between the divine and the living.

That Europeans feared Voodoo as a form of resistance to their rule can be seen in legal prohibitions of its practices and arrests of devotees, which were documented in newspaper accounts of its rituals: given Voodoo's ability "to empower the slave and free black population, the French, Spanish, and later, the American authorities in Louisiana sought to suppress" it (Dedek 122). In 1773, several enslaved people were charged with using gris-gris, a Voodoo charm, to kill a European slaveholder. Spanish authorities also restricted African funeral practices. In 1850, women who were "'slaves, free colored persons, and white persons" were arrested for "dancing Voudou'" (122). This biracial group had violated a Louisiana law that prohibited mixed-race and enslaved gatherings out of fear that such meetings would foment resistance to slavery and racism. The prominence of women priestesses in Voodoo also threatened white male supremacy, with numerous women arrested for practicing Voodoo before the Civil War. In turn, "the repression of Voodoo forced the religion underground, making it seem even more mysterious and threatening, but also fascinating and alluring to many whites and others" (123). As a result, the use of Voodoo by white slave owners was commonplace (Pile 78).

Celebrated in music, literature, television, and film, as well as a staple of walking tours, Marie Laveau is the most famous Voodoo priestess of all time. Her grave in St. Louis Cemetery #1 is still visited today: locals and tourists alike still attempt to mark her tomb with crosses in an effort to have their wishes heard and fulfilled (see figure 6). The subject of two major biographies in the early 2000s, she continues to fascinate. An influential figure in nineteenth-century New Orleans, Laveau's existence is documented by a few official documents and newspaper articles. That she existed and practiced Voodoo is not in doubt, but whether she had a daughter with whom she shared a name and Voodoo practices and whether she recanted her belief in Voodoo at the end of her life are un-

known. The two biographies by scholars Martha Ward and Carolyn Morrow Long offer conflicting accounts. The lack of documentation is unsurprising, given that practicing Voodoo was illegal and its rites and gatherings (due to their mixed-race composition) were banned during Laveau's lifetime; there were also reasons for her to stay in the shadows and avoid publicity.

Marie Laveau's existence, however, is acknowledged in newspaper obituaries and oral accounts of her life collected by the 1930s Works Progress Administration, whose staff interviewed seventy mostly African American respondents (Long, *Laveau*, xxiv–xxvi, 209). A record held by the Catholic Church attests that she and her children were practicing Catholics and that she was baptized and married in the city's St. Louis Cathedral (Ward 20). Laveau was both a Catholic and a Voodoo priestess, reflecting the early nineteenth-century fusion of cultures in New Orleans. But Voodoo offered women more power and authority than did the Catholic Church. In describing Voodoo's characteristics and the theory that there were two Marie Laveaus, a long-lived mother and then a daughter of the same name, anthropologist Martha Ward explains, "Voodoo, as the Laveaus practiced it, is one of many women's religions . . . women's religions are not set apart from the world's larger and better-known religions; they are an organic parallel, a female counterpart, a way to acknowledge women's experiences and losses" (99). Long points out that Laveau's influence and power were unusual for a free woman of color in a racially segregated city in the nineteenth century, but that "New Orleans voudou [Long uses this variant spelling] was primarily a religion of women dominated by priestesses who served a racially diverse, mostly female congregation" (118). Voodoo provided an expression of and continuation of African spiritual beliefs that were practiced not only by free people of color like Laveau but also by those who were enslaved, white, or of mixed race.

Just as there are accounts of two Marie Laveaus serving as influential Voodoo priestesses, there are also two competing sites that may be her grave. Long describes visiting the more likely grave in St. Louis Cemetery #1 and completing the expected ritual: "rap three times on the wall, draw a cross mark with a bit of soft red brick, place your hand on the marble slab, ask Marie to grant your wish, and leave a small offering of coins, fruit, candy, or flowers" (xv). Until his family moved his body to another larger family tomb in another cemetery, the city's first Black mayor, "Dutch" Morial, was buried near Laveau's tomb for twenty-five years. Some claim he wished to be buried there because he credited her for his success. Whether it is true or not, this story attests to the belief in her ongoing presence and influence.

New Orleans's cities of the dead play a powerful role in Voodoo, not for creating zombies, but for their dirt and dust used in spells and charms. And even though extreme, oppressive segregation became the law of the city after a brief respite during Reconstruction when federal troops enforced limited legal rights, the cemeteries themselves were never fully segregated. Because all ethnicities buried their dead together, the spiritual rites and practices of death mingled in these spaces. Whites were exposed to Voodoo and visited the same cemeteries that Voodoo believers did. Diverse spiritual beliefs mixed in cemeteries, strengthening the fusion of European and African supernatural beliefs and customs and making the supernatural even more powerful, enhanced by beliefs in Voodoo and ghosts: "The belief that spirits inhabited cemeteries and could be summoned to do one's bidding created a religious and spiritual link between the city of the living and the cities of the dead" (Dedek 124–125).

Documentation of Voodoo activities in New Orleans cemeteries and elsewhere continues to appear in local newspapers. On July 14, 2021, "a Voodoo priest was spotted at the Orleans Parish Criminal Court building hard at work cleansing the court's steps" (Tolliver 2021). The priest was scattering holy water and burning sage to purify the space where candidates for public office go to file paperwork to participate in upcoming elections. This public ritual suggests the ongoing fascination in and practice of Voodoo.

Belief in ghosts, by contrast, is not exclusive to Voodoo, although the concept that ghosts can and should be invoked in everyday life is. Ghosts serve a powerful function, as writer Toni Morrison shows in her novel *Beloved:* they are a powerful salve for the memory of those lost to tragic deaths and the horrors of slavery. Joseph Roach's *Cities of the Dead,* an analysis of performances in London and New Orleans, addresses the significance of ghosts for enslaved people. While discussing street performances by Black Mardi Gras Indians, Roach cites an important Native American spiritual belief that was widespread in the Great Plains and was brought to New Orleans via the traveling Buffalo Bill show. This show influenced the Black tradition of masking as Native Americans, which Roach describes as resisting the myth of Anglo-American entitlement by "re-enacting African American memory through the surrogation of Native American identities" (208). The Cheyenne Ghost Dance religion held that "if the Indians could keep dancing to the right spirit, their dead would return to life, and their world would be replenished and restored to them. White folly, an excrescent superabundance in America, would disappear" (207). Seeing the Mardi Gras Indians as a form of resistance to white supremacy evokes the concept not only of reanimated bodies or zombies but also of ghosts. Historically, ghosts appear when there are unresolved issues and injustices (Pulliam 2014; Roberts 2019). Unsurprisingly, many of the narratives about ghosts in New Orleans revolve around injustices of enslavement and racism.

The geographical fluidity of New Orleans's setting, its cultural heritage of Native American and African beliefs about the permeability between the living and the dead, its deadly and regular occurrences of disease, and the scourge of enslavement set up the city as a place of extraordinary supernatural happenings. Seeking escape or reassurance, stories about ghosts and supernatural beings often evoke retributive justice, a correction of the wrongs experienced by living people.

Voodoo Practitioners

Voodoo, as exemplified by the Voodoo queen Marie Laveau, is the focus of this book's second chapter for several reasons. First, Voodoo is an actual spiritual practice, conducted by real people from the past and present. It is the supernatural practice that is the most accessible, because its precepts are easy to understand and use everyday materials. Its impact was documented in the 1930s and 1940s by the Works Progress Administration (WPA) interviews conducted in the city: "Many of the WPA Slave Narratives contain accounts of healing practices, medicine plants, spiritual belief systems, and stories of origin. These topics are the same types of information of traditions and knowledge systems passed in verbal form, from generation to-generation, in other Indigenous cultural communities" (Moody 22). Voodoo's practice in New Orleans is a part of documented history, and New Orleans is the city most associated with it through the historical personage of Marie Laveau. Her legacy lives on not only in rituals and in commerce but also through the priestess as a figure in fiction, television, film, and numerous supernatural-focused walking tours. In this analysis, I focus on the Voodoo priestess rather than zombies. The shambling dead are inherently less interesting and have less power and agency than Voodoo priestesses. Zombies can be dangerous, but they are also a more important practice in Haitian Vodou than the fusion/hybrid that is New Orleans Voodoo. The New Orleans Voodoo tradition reduced the number of Haiti's supernatural figures, placed more emphasis on feminine powers, and saw the Voodoo priestesses as vital conduits who could bring the divine into the world of the living through sacrifice and ritual.

As a commanding female figure who wielded power in a society where people of color were enslaved and where even those who were free endured rampant discrimination, Voodoo priestess Marie Laveau resisted white supremacy, misogyny, and traditional patriarchal religion. The historical Marie Laveau ministered to those in prison, offering them comfort when she could not free them. She gave women the opportunity to address their concerns and provided potions and spiritual knowledge to them. In rituals described as being orgiastic, she created a space where women could dance and celebrate their bodies in a world where their bodies were rigidly policed. For example, women of color were denied the right to wear hats and bonnets, so that their attire could be a marker of their second-class status. Creating elaborate scarf headdresses or tignons was a way that nineteenth-century women defied the prohibitions, showing that they could use their skill and artistry to craft becoming and beautiful headwear. Although we have no images of Marie Laveau, she likely appeared as a free woman of color in several famous portraits, her hair in a tignon. In the same way that she wore a tignon and subverted white supremacist society's attempt to contain her, so she offered an alternative worldview to whites, Blacks (free and enslaved), women, and men. Although she did not engage in direct conflict with white society, she challenged its dominance.

The historical Marie Laveau died almost one hundred and fifty years ago, but her presence lives on in those who practice Voodoo.

As S. Frederick Starr noted in 1985, in New Orleans, "Organized voodoo is a thing of the past, but more than a few do-it-yourself practitioners live on" (167). Osbey's recent essay, "Why We Can't Talk to You about Voodoo," highlights its ongoing presence, albeit a secretive one, in New Orleans. Criticizing the appropriation of Voodoo by whites and tourists, Osbey explains that "the religion here in New Orleans is entirely within the sphere of women, whom we call Mothers" (4). Sallie Ann Glassman, who is of Jewish Ukrainian heritage, is a prominent Voodoo priestess in New Orleans who runs a Voodoo shop in the city; she is one of the few priestesses with a public profile who has been trained in Haitian Vodou and who initiates others. There are at least seven Voodoo establishments in the city, including Marie Laveau's House of Voodoo, Bloody Mary's Tours at the Haunted Museum and Voodoo Shop, the Voodoo Bone Lady Voodoo Shop, Erzulie's Shop, Esoterica Occult Goods, Crescent City Conjure, and Voodoo Authentica. Numerous walking tours in the city focus on Voodoo, and cemetery tours feature Laveau's tomb in St. Louis Cemetery #1. Dozens of other tours that boast names such as "Haunted History" and "French Quarter Phantoms" include Voodoo with a focus on Laveau. The popular television series *American Horror Story: Coven* also features this Voodoo priestess.

Even before that popular series aired in 2013, most French Quarter walking tours stopped at the Madame LaLaurie mansion. Although there is no historical evidence that LaLaurie and Marie Laveau knew each other, the television show posits an intense rivalry and conflict between them, which has also stoked interest in Laveau. (Spoiler, Laveau wins and is a heroine.) Voodoo figures in the plot of many television shows set in New Orleans; invariably, the episodes seem to endorse Voodoo's validity as a practice. A 1980s groundbreaking dramedy TV show set in New Orleans, *Frank's Place* takes as its premise that Voodoo is strong enough to compel a Boston college professor to relocate to New Orleans against his will. In an episode titled "Dueling Voodoo," the professor is in a tug of war between two female Voodoo practitioners, having hired one to evict the other from a house he owns. In an episode of *Bones* titled "The Man in the Morgue," set in the city just after Hurricane Katrina, the normally fact-based forensic scientist Temperance Brennan finds herself ensnared in a Voodoo murder, with the show endorsing the reality of the religion.

Marie Laveau also lives on in songs and fiction. Numerous popular songs focus on Voodoo, either citing her directly, as with Dr. Hook and the Medicine Show's "Marie Laveau" (1974) and "Witch Queen of New Orleans" by Redbone (1971), or indirectly in songs such as Muddy Waters's "Got My Mojo Working" (1960) or "Black Magic Woman" by Santana (1970), to name just a few examples. These and other Voodoo songs have been covered by numerous bands, and Voodoo continues to appear in popular music around the world in hits like "Voodoo Song" in French by Willy Williams (2017). The lyrics emphasize the power and sensuality of Voodoo, with Williams's song highlighting a young Black girl using Voodoo to make even a dour security cop break into dance.

Jewell Parker Rhodes's *Voodoo Dreams* and a subsequent trilogy of mystery novels, as well as a novel by Francine Prose titled *Marie Laveau*, are perhaps the best-known works of fiction to feature her. The Voodoo priestess is also a character in many other New Orleans–set fictions, such as Barbara Hambly's series of Benjamin January detective novels. Rhodes's *Voodoo Dreams* imagines Laveau's life from early girlhood to her rise to power, filling in imaginatively what little exists in the historical record. The novel has been described as an example of "Voodoo feminism" by scholar Tara Green, a characterization that emphasizes the resistant quality of Laveau's life and legacy.

These cultural performances and texts draw most directly on Marie Laveau, but many, like "Dueling Voodoo," focus on its continuing spiritual practices. New Orleans's reluctance to embrace corporate capitalism, its notoriously lax political practices, and pleasure-seeking reputation—its motto is "laissez les bon temps roulez" (let the good times roll)—have helped cement the city's reputation as "the Caribbean's northernmost city." New Orleans's traditional Catholicism with its emphasis on ritual, including the yearly Mardi Gras "farewell to the flesh," tolerates Voodoo and alternative spiritual beliefs, just as the church did in ancient times with pagan rituals. The New Orleans tourism industry has capitalized on the city's association with Voodoo in numerous ads and marketing campaigns, and in the many Voodoo shops and walking tours in the French Quarter alone. The city's excessive number of cemeteries provides material for Voodoo rituals that require grave dust, respect for the dead, and engagement with them in the world of the living.

Ghosts

If the city's connection to Voodoo can be traced to one Voodoo priestess, its association with ghosts can be tied to its high death rates and many victims of disease—yellow fever, dengue fever, and malaria—as well as of brutal conditions of enslavement, wars, poor sanitation, floods, fires, and hurricanes. That so many of the city's residents revered their ancestors and saw them as actors in the world of the living also encouraged a belief in ghosts. The tiny house-like tombs in which New Orleanians are buried offer a space where even today people can readily envision ghosts. Spared the destruction of its spectacular nineteenth-century housing, the French Quarter, the Garden District, and other centuries-old areas of New Orleans offer many structures perfect for ghosts to haunt because, as living beings, they suffered and died there; for example, a hotel that served as a Civil War hospital and one that had housed a school that caught fire are haunted by their former inhabitants. One French Quarter restaurant even reserves a table for the ghosts haunting its space (see figure 7). There are also ghosts who suffered the cruelties of enslavement and white supremacy, such as the Black female ghost desperate to wed her white married lover mentioned at the beginning of this chapter. Madame LaLaurie's

FIG. 7. A table for a ghost at Muriel's Restaurant.
Photograph by the author.

French Quarter mansion still stands: the notorious site of torture and mass murder of the Black people she enslaved is the final stop on many supernatural history tours.

Ghosts are more passive than Voodoo priestesses who challenge white supremacy and hope to affect the living through rituals and spells. But even though ghosts rarely act in the living world, their presence alone acts as a protest against injustice. Customarily, the reason why ghosts hang around is to resolve issues around their violent deaths: they may have been denied revenge or acknowledgment of the horror of what happened to them. By haunting the site where they were killed or suffered, ghosts demand attention, demand that their stories be told. Thus, understanding the stories of ghosts in New Orleans provides insight into the city's history and its many victims.

Like the world of Voodoo, the world of ghosts tends to be dominated by females: for every account of a male soldier ghost, there are two or three more of female ghosts. Even if the ghost itself is male, it is feminized. Often unseen and unheard, and nearly invisible if seen, the ghost occupies a marginal space in the world of the supernatural as its least powerful figure. Certainly less powerful in the afterlife than a Voodoo priestess, who has almost deity-like powers to grant wishes, the ghost hangs around, often unable to speak. Although poltergeists, a type of ghost, can move objects, most are limited to sound and light effects. They ask only that we recognize that they existed. Privileged by their shadowy, ambiguous position in between life and death, ghosts parallel the geography of New Orleans, both water- and land-based, and thus liminal and shifting.

Fiction that focuses on New Orleans ghosts use the history of the city to explain why spirits are more present in this city than any other. Many folklore accounts set in New Orleans feature ghosts and were collected by Jeanne deLavigne and published in *Ghost Stories of Old New Orleans;* in response to the continuing interest in New Orleans's spirits, this book was reprinted in 2013. It tells of Civil War ghosts, but more prevalent are women who were scorned, neglected, and often murdered and who cannot leave where they were treated so badly. *Bridge of Souls,* a book in the best-selling young adult ghost-hunter series by Victoria Schwab, is set in New Orleans. The ghosts that Cassidy, the novel's adolescent protagonist, encounters are mostly female. As her ghost-hunting parents shoot a television show about ghosts, Cassidy is the one who encounters real ghosts, learning about why they continue to haunt. In many instances, she offers them release and escape from their entrapment in the city. As she learns about the history of the city and specific tragedies, Cassidy realizes that ghosts want most of all to be seen and heard. New Orleans's ghosts, who in real life were marginalized and excised from official histories, crave recognition.

The ghosts that haunt Madame LaLaurie's mansion at the corner of Royal and Governor Nicholls St. in New Orleans are the focus of many haunted history tours, as well as television fictions like *American Horror Story: Coven.* Accounts from 1834 confirm that enslaved people were tortured and murdered at this site in practices so vile that they outraged the city's populace. One story recounts that when a young enslaved girl flung herself from a roof, LaLaurie was charged with illegal abuse and forced to pay a fine. Later that year, another enslaved person started a fire, further revealing the heinous crimes of Madame LaLaurie when the authorities entered the home to extinguish the flames. LaLaurie and her husband fled as a mob gathered; they were never held accountable for their terrible crimes. The mansion was vacant for more than forty years, during which time screams and cries were often heard emanating from the abandoned structure. Later in the nineteenth century as immigrants flooded the French Quarter, several families moved into the house, unaware of its history. But all soon left after describing unbearable screams and hauntings by the enslaved people's ghosts. The building was subsequently used as a furniture warehouse until poltergeists began to damage the goods stored there, leaving bloody messes; the warehouse was soon vacated. Eventually Nicholas Cage bought the building to renovate and stay in on his many trips to New Orleans. Cage has a special connection to New Orleans: not only is he fascinated by the supernatural, but he also designed and had constructed an elaborate above-ground tomb for himself in St. Louis Cemetery #1. Now owned by a couple from California, the creepy mansion is often decorated for Halloween with plastic skeletons and groaning figures with flashing lights. But the cheesy overcoating of the supernatural is challenged every night, as dozens of walking tours spend several minutes listening to their guides elaborate on the horrors and hauntings said to still take place in this building.

The historian and biographer of Madame LaLaurie is herself a skeptic of ghosts, but there are almost two hundred years of documents of negative, upsetting, and even tragic incidents associated with the LaLaurie mansion. Identifying contemporary documents that support the reporting and even criminal charges levied against Madame LaLaurie for abuse and torture, Long demonstrates that even in a time when it was legal to own and abuse people, LaLaurie's actions were seen as atrocities (*LaLaurie*, 85–88). It is assumed that the primary abuser was the madame, which makes her an exception to the mostly male abusers. If not in life, she is at least punished for her crimes in the fictional *American Horror Story: Coven*.

This most notorious of haunted houses exemplifies the classic case of ghosts whose terrible mistreatment was ignored while they were alive. The immensely wealthy LaLauries were not chastened by fines for excessive abuse of their enslaved servants. Nor did the enslaved ever receive justice, and indeed, except for nineteen people who were identified by Long, their names have long been lost (*LaLaurie*, 144).

Vampires

If ghosts ask the living to remember past suffering and to acknowledge and correct injustice, vampires offer a bloody embodiment: they are a metaphor for the exploitation of humans by humans. Although vampire myths are found in African and Asian folklore, the modern Western obsession with the vampire was generated by Bram Stoker's *Dracula*. In that novel, Dracula is drawn from his native Transylvania to London, a sprawling, diverse city and center of an exploitative colonial empire. This urban space offered him anonymity and more victims, as well as a chance to create more vampires. The vampire's predatory exploitation of humans, drinking their blood to maintain its immortal life, made it an even better metaphor for New Orleans, which, unlike London, had not yet made slavery illegal. Even after slavery ended, the continuation of white supremacy in the city (and nation) meant that the metaphor of vampirism as white people's exploitation of other human beings still reverberated. New Orleans's legalization of prostitution in the district known as Storyville from 1898 until 1917 also dovetails with the representation of the female seductress, sucking blood from her enthralled victim. More generally, the representation of the city as "Wicked New Orleans" and the "Big Easy" suggests that it was a place that ignored the bestial and violent, and this view is corroborated by its history. As Steve Pile notes, while cities offer a perfect haven for vampires, "one of the main cities attracting vampire attention is New Orleans" (100). Part of New Orleans's unique appeal is its "long association with vampire myths" (117).

The figure of the vampire has also been appropriated as a stand-in for people who enslaved other humans. In works like George R. R. Martin's *Fevre Dream,* vampires exploit humanity's evil system of slavery so they can engage more easily in their own practice of drinking human blood. But in Martin's novel and in other works of fiction, the vampire's predation always appears as less evil and more justifiable than the brutal practices of slavery. The vampire, after all, requires blood to survive, whereas the enslavement of humans by humans was a financial calculation to generate profit. Once the largest slave market in the South, New Orleans is thus an appropriate place for actual vampires to locate. Historically depicted as having an aristocratic upbringing and being elegant and urbane, the vampire gravitated to cities, with New Orleans's well-known tolerance of debauchery and diversity allowing the creature more cover.

New Orleans's reputation as a site for vampires draws not only on its having the highest death rate per capita during the nineteenth century but also on its character as one of the United States' most European cities. Its unique architecture of alleys, wrought-iron balconies, and old, beautiful, but often decrepit buildings provides an ideal atmosphere for vampires to thrive. The innumerable fictional portrayals of New Orleans as the abode of vampires have left their mark. In the city you can find "fangsmiths" who create artificial fangs, the Vampire Café serving blood-inspired crafted cocktails, a vampire shop, many vampire tours, and vampire performers. The downtown Mardi Gras parade Chewbacchus includes marchers from the Vampire Council of New Orleans. Slightly campy but impeccably costumed down to fangs, the paraders distribute doubloons bearing their organization name and stickers. A young man in formal wear and fangs displays a typical performance of a vampire (see figure 8). New Orleans also hosts an annual Vampire Film Fest, and its huge Halloween celebrations attract many vampire costumers. As a convention city, New Orleans is a favored and frequent site of vampire conventions.

There *are* humans who identify as vampires, and a recent study of vampire communities did focus on the Big Easy. Like non-vampiristic residents, self-proclaimed New Orleans vampires were found to differ from those in other cities by their indifference to events outside the city. The author of a study on this community, John Edgar Browning, notes, "The French Quarter, the central research site . . . is particularly germane to this line of inquiry" (4). It was in French Quarter haunts such as Wicked New Orleans (a goth shop, now closed) and a bar named The Dungeon that the researcher found self-identified vampires (5). He found them burned, not by exposure to the sun's rays, but by what they considered an unfair depiction of their community on the ABC news magazine program, *20/20*, which aired in 2009. Author Steve Pile also encountered a "real-life vampire" named Vlad Tepes Knight on a Haunted History Tour.

Researching her book *Spirits of New Orleans,* Kala Ambrose encountered numerous ghosts, but her most chilling encounter was a vampire sighting. While on a carriage ride in the French Quar-

FIG. 8. Jack, a vampire on Royal Street, at Café Lafitte in exile.
Photograph by the author.

ter, she experienced a paralyzing chill, a "cold forbidding energy" (76) that the vampire exuded, who was attempting to keep her from escaping him. Ambrose has since discussed this creature with other researchers, and she credits the carriage's mule with struggling and redirecting the vehicle, allowing them all to get away. She concludes, "I have never felt this type of energy again, and I can offer no proof of the existence of vampires beyond my personal experience, which I know to be real and authentic" (77). Further historical research and consultation allowed her to identify the vampire as a historical figure, Jacques St. Germain, who lived in the area in 1902. Suspected in the deaths of several women, he disappeared mysteriously, and rumors of his becoming a vampire began to circulate. Ambrose's experience and the ability to connect it with a historical New Orleans figure offer a perfect example of the connection between the city's past and its present. The figure of the vampire is kept alive not only through fiction but also through people's accounts of their experiences of the supernatural in the city.

The "Casket Girls" were involved in yet another vampire story told in modern times but based on early New Orleans events (see figure 9). When France was unable to recruit sufficient colonists for New Orleans—the first white colonists had a miserable time, with many dying and those who survived having to rely on Native American knowledge and support—it dispatched prisoners and women who had been convicted of crimes, including prostitution, to the colony. Concerned about these criminals' effect on the colony, which from the beginning was not only physically inhospitable but also a place of lawlessness, the French authorities recruited convent-educated young women and sent them with dowries and three nun chaperones to be courted and married legally to the men of the city; before being married off, the young women were kept under lock and key in the Ursuline Convent. Their dowries were packaged in small wooden boxes called "caskets" in French. The name given to the boxes and the fact that the young women were locked up by the nuns gave rise to stories of female vampires. If vampires are about exploitation of others and power, the fact that women could legally own property in the colony also explains the development of this vampire legend.

According to this tale, one group of young women arrived, like the other Casket Girls, by ship and went to the convent. But their "caskets" were full sized and locked tight, not to be opened until

FIG. 9. *Embarkment of the Casket Girls.*
Courtesy of the Historic New Orleans Collection, Acc. no. 1974.25.10.39.

each woman left the convent to be married. This detail about the size and security of the chests encouraged the idea that the women were vampires sleeping in the "caskets." One night, a curious nun opened one box, only to discover that it was empty. Deciding that the caskets had contained vampires, the nuns blessed thousands of screws and then had all the upstairs windows screwed shut. Nevertheless, the wind blew open the windows, and they had to be closed again and sealed many times. Ambrose, who recounts the most detailed version of this tale in her book, states unequivocally that the vampires in the coffins were female and that they "created a powerful new lineage of vampires in the city" (105). Steve Pile also recounts the tale, adding that "speculation is that these women [vampires] are still there, sealed and concealed on the upper floor of the convent" (127). That the Ursuline Convent building—a National Historic Landmark identified as a singular example of French Colonial architecture in the lower Mississippi Valley—is still in use today adds to the mystique.

Not only the history but also the geography of New Orleans, then, contributes to making the city the abode of Voodoo, ghosts, and vampires (see figure 10). Writer and supernatural expert Kala Ambrose notes that New Orleans's nickname, the Crescent City, evokes its feminized nature: the land has "a chalice shape which represents feminine energies . . . [and] one of the properties of the feminine is psychic powers." According to Ambrose, the city "serves as a natural vortex where magic and mysterious happenings can take place" (http://aidyreviews.net/spirits-of-new-orleans -review). Kalila Katherina Smith, author of *Ghosts and Vampires of New Orleans,* claims that "the actual history of New Orleans is far stranger than anything fictional writers can create. These stories have been documented by paranormal investigations, police reports, personal accounts, as well as our city's archives" (4). Whether the three supernatural types introduced in this chapter are real or not, I leave up to the reader to decide. But by exploring the representation of Voodoo priestesses, ghosts, and vampires, we can learn not only about the tensions, struggles, and dangers of life in New Orleans for more than three hundred years but also about why the supernatural still haunts us. If nothing else, it is my hope that readers of this book will travel to New Orleans for the first time to see for themselves, or return to the city to see it through the eyes of its supernatural inhabitants.

FIG. 10. The French Quarter in the fog. It is easy to imagine a Voodoo queen, a ghost, or a vampire here. Photograph by Valerie Esparza.

2

FEMININE POWER
AND NEW ORLEANS'S
VOODOO QUEEN

x x x

There is no name that conjures up
voodoo in New Orleans like
that of Marie Laveau.

—TROY TAYLOR

In my many visits to the city's Voodoo shops, I feel the energy
and power in their items for sale. Cute, brightly colored Voodoo dolls with large stitches are too obviously kitschy tourist
souvenirs, but the large jars of mysterious herbs and powders and
the African masks and statues command attention. As the staff
will tell you, trying to wield any power is fraught with danger and
requires knowledge. Although I have often been tempted to purchase something from a Voodoo shop, my respect for the power of
this religion has stayed my hand.

Voodoo is inextricably part of the city of New Orleans, as
Kodi L. Roberts shows in the clever opening of his 2015 book *Voodoo and Power: The Politics of Religion in New Orleans, 1881–1940*.
Using a detailed description of two Super Bowl ads focusing on
Voodoo, Roberts explores the ways that popular culture identifies
it as an essential feature of the city. Examining decades of popular
culture depictions of Voodoo, this chapter illustrates the depth and
complexity of the religion's place in New Orleans.

Beginning with a 1998 episode of *Frank's Place* titled "Dueling
Voodoo," this chapter explores representations of New Orleans

Voodoo in literature, television, film, and the city's many walking tours. These various accounts of Voodoo are anchored in the figure of Marie Laveau, who gained power and notoriety while the enslavement of people of color was legal. Jewell Parker Rhodes's critically acclaimed and compelling 1993 novel, *Voodoo Dreams: A Novel of Marie Laveau,* reveals Laveau's feminist legacy that Tara Green, in her analysis of Rhodes's fiction, describes as "voodoo feminism" (283). This emphasis on female empowerment appears in *American Horror Story: Coven* (2013–2014) and in the city's numerous walking tours that feature Voodoo. Critical to Voodoo's representation is its history, even though for a variety of reasons, including its legal prohibition, the documentation of Voodoo is sparse. Yet newspaper and ethnographic accounts agree that Voodoo was a practice that was respected and feared and that its preeminent practitioner was the Voodoo queen Marie Laveau.

Zombies are antithetical to New Orleans Voodoo's emphasis on love and liberation. Instead, the undead are the ancestors and gods on whom a Voodoo practitioner could call for help. In addition to their powers as intercessors for the living, Voodoo priestesses would also channel the gods, especially Papa Legba, who himself was a conduit between the living and the gods. A python snake symbolizes his power, and Laveau would dance with one, compelling and, at times, putting her audience into a trance—again a liminal state between life and death.

Some Voodoo rituals in the city are open to the public, especially around All Hallows' Eve. In contrast to the commercialization and marketing of Voodoo by walking tours and most of the Voodoo shops, these events demonstrate Voodoo's spiritual and positive aspects. On October 31, Voodoo Authentica of the New Orleans Cultural Center & Collection, a Voodoo practitioner–owned establishment that city residents vouch for as a place of "real" Voodoo, presents VOODOOFEST (www.voodoofest.com) annually, which is open to the public and free of charge. An all-day event, the festival features several Voodoo priestesses, musical performances and dances, and educational talks about Voodoo

FIG. 11. Voodoo priestess Ava Kay Jones at VOODOOFEST.
Photograph by Ann Witucki.

and Catholicism, as well as African and African American culture
(see figure 11); it concludes with an ancestral healing ritual. Family
members of the shop owner make Creole food, from gumbo to
jambalaya, and share this bounty free of charge with the attendees.
This fest has been held for the last twenty-five years on the block
where the shop is located.

Brandi C. Kelley, the owner of Voodoo Authentica and an initiated Voodoo priestess, "remains a Catholic and says that New
Orleans Voodoo is a gumbo of African, Haitian, and New Orleans
traditions" (Johnson 2019). Similarly, Ann Witucki, a resident of

the nearby St. Roch neighborhood who attended the 2022 event, is a practicing Catholic. She was particularly impressed by a presentation by Voodoo priestess and native New Orleanian Ava Kay Jones, who spoke about what it means to be a "Voodoo Catholic." This integrative spiritual approach is endorsed by Witucki, who wears a necklace with a yellow pepper given to her by a friend for protection (as used in Voodoo). Her emotional response to the closing ancestral healing ritual illustrates the appeal and power of Voodoo, even for nonpractitioners. As the drummers increased the intensity and volume of their playing, Kelley reminded the audience that "the veil [between the world of the living and the dead] is thin. Time to shout out to our ancestors or anyone you want to reach." Witucki felt a rush of emotion, as the ritual helped her release her sadness caused by the death that very morning of a beloved family dog. Similarly, the event photographer Ellen Rosenberg was moved to put down her camera and join in with the drummers.

The experience of reaching out and letting go was heightened by rituals held earlier that day. One involved sweeping one's hands overhead in a gesture meant to clear the mind. In another ritual, a small fire was lit on the street that generated a spiritual cleansing/ blessing: some walked through the fire, and others jumped over it. As the drumming died down, people began to drift away, the special day's purpose having been acknowledged and achieved. A portrait of a free woman of color wearing a tignon—a painting often identified incorrectly as an actual portrait of the Voodoo queen— was propped up against the wall. Its effect was that Laveau was overseeing the day's events.

Another Voodoo event held annually on the next day, All Saints' Day, is led by priestess Sallie Ann Glassman—one of the few white women initiated into Haitian Vodou who has been practicing Voodoo in New Orleans since 1977 (https://www.islandofsalvationbo tanica.com). Among other public rituals, Glassman leads the Fet Gede Festival, or Festival of the Dead; it is held outside Glassman's shop, the Island of Salvation Botanica, which is housed in the New

Orleans Healing Center several blocks from the French Quarter. An altar sits just outside the shop's entryway with a large statue representing Laveau. Fet Gede honors the dead in a three-hour ceremony of drumming, singing, dancing, and the drawing of ritual signs (*veve*) to attract the spirits. There are usually about one hundred participants, including initiated priestesses and drummers, many from other houses of Voodoo worship; believers; and members of the public. Special attention is given to honoring and remembering family and friends who died during the past year; individuals proffer gifts to the loa (a spirit)—in this instance, Gede—and place a photo or other mementos of the deceased on the altar. An example of the overlapping of supernatural figures in New Orleans is the appearance at this ritual of vampire Father Sebastiaan, "a Master Fangsmith, published author, and Impresario of the Endless Night Vampire Ball" (fathersebastiaan.com). A commanding figure, Father Sebastiaan travels between Paris and cities in the United States. At the Fet Gede, however, he takes second place to the Voodoo adherents. In addition to this festival, Glassman leads the annual summer Hurricane Turning Ritual asking Our Lady of Prompt Succor and Ezili Danto for protection from hurricanes. These two events are open to the public, but many others take place privately in the city. Glassman is also well known for having designed her own set of New Orleans Voodoo tarot cards, one of which features Laveau.

Voodoo's emphasis on female practitioners—*voodooiennes* or Voodoo queens—suits the Crescent City's own identity as a feminized space. As William S. Woods explains in an article in *Modern Language Notes*, "Etymologically the name *Orleans* should be masculine in French . . . yet the name of the American city has apparently been feminine in French since its existence" (259–260). Presented as existing outside the capitalist economy and values of mainstream America (as represented by corporations, efficiency, and rationality), New Orleans is depicted as possessing an alternative culture, characterized by strong female figures and female-dominated Voodoo. As the defeated region in the American Civil

War, the South took on a subordinate, feminine role to the indus-
trialized, masculine North. That role has been reinforced by the
"white flight" of elites from the urban core of cities, leaving cities
marginalized and embodying the feminine through the poor and
disenfranchised. Author Grace King described New Orleans in
1915 as "among cities, the most feminine of women" (xvi). Almost a
hundred years later, writing in the *Wall Street Journal,* Douglas Mc-
Collam characterized New Orleans as "America's most feminine
city" (quoted in Hemard, "New Orleans," 3). These authors use
gendering to represent the allure of the city and the adjective "feminine" to mean both "other" and seductive and appealing. Thus,
New Orleans's feminization explains its ability to offer a positive experience and perspective that differs from those of other U.S. cities.

Not without reason is New Orleans frequently characterized as
the United States' "most European city" or the "northernmost Caribbean city" (Spera 2). Both those foreign locales stand in relation
to the United States as politically and symbolically feminine: they
are seen as indolent, relaxed, nonaggressive, and insufficiently concerned with capitalism. Roger D. Abrahams calls on his readers "to
visualize the city . . . as the crown of the Caribbean" (1). His evocative description focuses on New Orleans's combinations of cultures: "Conserving styles from a multitude of Old Worlds—from
west, central, and southern Africa, from many strains of Europe,
including Spain, France, Scotland, and their New World outcomes
in Cuba, Mexico, and Canada . . . New Orleans culture provides
a stylistic synthesis . . . founded on Latinate libertine populism
leavened with African styled performances" (9). Similarly, in an
interview in *Antigravity,* a monthly alternative magazine produced
in New Orleans, the film director John Waters describes New Orleans's separation from the rest of the United States: "New Orleans
does not participate in America. . . . It is a separate island away
from the rest of America. And I think most people in New Orleans
are quite happy with that" (Hill 22). Jazz, which emerged from its
legalized red-light district known as Storyville, and the city's tolerance and embrace of the pleasures of sex and alcohol created

its reputation for decadence and decay. An early jazz song, "Basin Street Blues"—its title marking a street in the most prestigious section of Storyville that was lined with beautiful mansions—calls New Orleans the "Land of Dreams" (Abrahams 8). One of the city's most important dreams, as indicated in Rhodes's novel, is "Voodoo Dreams."

The city's feminine aura made it an ideal setting for Voodoo. Its appeal for New Orleanians, especially during the nineteenth century, stemmed from the pain, misery, and injustice of a white supremacist, patriarchal society. Those who were oppressed and had no protection under the legal system had to look elsewhere to rebalance a system that denied their full humanity. As Kodi Roberts notes, not only enslaved Africans and African Americans but also free people of color and white people, especially white women, turned to Voodoo. Nineteenth-century accounts record more than one white male plantation owner who feared and employed Voodoo (Roberts 22–23, 34, 35).

Even though supernatural beings and powers often appear as threats to humans, there is a long-standing tradition in New Orleans of viewing otherworldly experiences and practices in a positive light. Especially for groups who are marginalized in a white heteronormative patriarchal society, the supernatural can offer solace and is "portrayed as an ultimately positive, ennobling force, causing or catalyzing a welcome development. Encounters with the supernatural are ultimately not sources of fear or malice and tend to leave protagonists transformed in some way" (MacDonald 94). Though MacDonald writes about Scottish women writers, her ideas are applicable to the use of Voodoo by other female writers, people of color, and the LGBTQ+ community. In a discussion of Julia Kristeva's analysis of writing and the birth process, MacDonald identifies the use of the semiotic as parallel to the division between the real world and the afterlife/supernatural world. Privileging the semiotic and the supernatural results in "a kind of second birth, renewal and development for the protagonists, and subsequently for readers" (95).

Frank's Place, "Dueling Voodoo"

Although it only aired for one season, the award-winning television series *Frank's Place* (1986–1987) had a compelling impact because of its focus on African American culture. It was the first show to depict New Orleans's Black culture with depth and accuracy, focusing, among other topics, on African American social clubs, food traditions, and spiritual beliefs. It also was the first TV show to take a folkloric approach to New Orleans's beliefs and practices relating to death and the supernatural. Although the show's title character is male, his three guides to the supernatural folk practices of the city are Black women: his girlfriend, an older Black employee of his restaurant, and a Voodoo doctor. These characters and their actions are based on research on the city by the series's showrunners.

Although LaShawn Harris's book *Sex Workers, Psychics, and Numbers Runners* focuses on New York City, her exploration of Black women's historical association with the supernatural has relevance for my analysis of *Frank's Place*. In both, the Black women are part of "an established tradition of African American women who claimed to possess supernatural abilities . . . during the antebellum era, some enslaved and some free black women were considered conjurers, root workers, and practitioners of magic, often fusing African rituals, traditions, and worldview with that of Anglo-American religion" (95). Citing observations of Black women made by the nineteenth-century abolitionist William Wells Brown and the actress Frances Kemble, among others, Harris stresses both the power and importance of the supernatural to enslaved people and its acknowledgment by white outsiders. She explains, "The supernatural world was integral to the creation of resistance strategies against the system of slavery . . . [including] providing some with the courage and opportunity to run away and to defy slave owners" (96). Tracing the persistence of belief in the supernatural to the twentieth century, Harris claims that many African Americans "believed that hoodoo and conjure practices and other supernatural rituals and paraphernalia were potentially beneficial to their daily lives" (96). Practicing Voodoo as a profession was "one of the few underground occupations that enabled black women to forge distinct spaces for themselves" (97).

Voodoo practitioners respect their ancestors, and it is this belief that shapes Frank's experience with the practice. The Black women he consults urge him to follow in the path of his deceased father and begin running the community restaurant. A university professor from Boston who specializes in the European Renaissance, Frank has not been in New Orleans since he was two years old. He never knew his father and comes to New Orleans intending to sell the restaurant and the other property he inherited from his recently deceased dad. When he has no legal recourse to evict a woman who has been terrifying his other tenants in rental property inherited from his father, Frank, as the landlord, must turn to a Voodoo practitioner for assistance. In this instance, the benign Voodoo priestess does not commune with a god to bring about a resolution but instead uses her knowledge and abilities to create a powerful potion. Voodoo brings Frank the wisdom and courage to act that he is unable to summon on his own behalf.

In its acceptance of Voodoo as legitimate and effective, the series endorses it as a powerful religion. That Frank is a well-educated Yankee who nevertheless uses Voodoo to solve his problems shows the impact of his move to New Orleans. A community leader because of his position as owner of a restaurant serving the African American community, Frank functions as a role model, including in his conversion to Voodoo. You might be skeptical or not believe in the supernatural, the series implies, but if you come to New Orleans, you will have a chance to experience it for yourself.

The very premise of *Frank's Place* reflects what Joseph Roach calls "surrogation": how a culture reproduces and recreates itself through repeated performances of folklore, providing a means by which it maintains what its participants consider "authenticity." Many episodes in the series illustrate this concept: key female characters act to ensure that Frank takes over his father's restaurant, though, as Roach notes about surrogation generally, not entirely satisfactorily (2). Significantly, the female characters create the surrogation through what Mary Belenky and her coauthors describe in their book of the same title as "women's ways of knowing." In the preface to the 1986 edition of their book (published just before *Frank's Place* aired), they describe "the ways of knowing that women have cultivated and learned to value, ways that we have come to believe are powerful but have been neglected by the dominant intellectual ethos of our time" (xxvii). The female characters educate Frank in this feminine alternative way of knowing, grounded in the African American community's beliefs and practices.

Frank's biological mother is not part of the series and perhaps is deceased; in her place, the elderly Miss Marie, a long-time employee of the restaurant, steps in to guide and direct Frank into his new role. She explains to the lawyer Bubba that "I can't die until Frank learns the business. The Lord told me so" ("Disengaged"). The other waitress, Anna Mae, reminds Miss Marie, "The boy's got to learn, just like you said" ("Frank Takes Charge"). The show's female characters demonstrate their "constructed knowledge"; they see "knowledge as contextual and experience themselves as creators of knowledge" (Belenky et al. 15). Anna Mae even steps in to translate for Frank when he has trouble understanding the cook Shorty's Cajun pronunciation ("Frank Takes Charge").

Several of Frank's informants are female: in addition to Miss Marie and Anna Mae, there are Hanna Griffin and her mother, Bertha Griffin-Lamour, who owns the funeral home where Hanna works. Throughout the show, these women and others employ folk practices to inform, educate, and guide Frank. Their tutelage is one way that New Orleans reifies "the commonly accepted stereotype of women's thinking as emotional and intuitive . . . [in contrast to] Western technologically oriented cultures which value rationality and objectivity" (Belenky et al. 6). In contrast to the Northern, rational mode of being, New Orleans offers what Yankee-raised Frank Parrish perceives to be a nonrational, intuitive mode of existence. He begins his initiation into New Orleans culture when he changes his mind about selling his father's property to the highest bidder and instead decides to care for the people who worked for his father. In following his father's practice of seeing workers as part of his family, Frank functions as his father's surrogate. In accepting the alternative reality that the city offers, the main character and the show's viewers begin to see and appreciate its unique features.

The pilot episode of *Frank's Place*, "Frank's Return," makes gendered associations with New Orleans's cultural identity clear. After his parents separated when he was two, Frank never saw his father again and had presumed his father was deceased. Meeting the restaurant employees for the first time, Frank states his intention to sell the restaurant and use the money to travel to Europe. Dressed in a suit and perspiring heavily from the heat, Frank Parrish is an outsider, literally uncomfortable in New Orleans. He asks, "Is it always this hot here?" and admits, "I don't know anything about New Orleans." Frank requires education to adapt to what will become his new home. From the pilot episode on, the series emphasizes New Orleans's differences from the rest of the world. Even its laws are different, as the lawyer Bubba explains: "The way Louisiana inheritance laws work, you, as the only son, get everything." Miss Marie, the matriarch of the restaurant, tells the staff and Frank that he must run the restaurant. Her words contain the show's title: "This is Frank's Place," and "this is where he belongs." She has a way, Voodoo, to ensure that Frank will stay.

In several episodes, the protagonist Frank wrestles with strong female figures and a feminine aesthetic that challenges his patriarchal beliefs. These figures and belief systems are presented as "Other" to Frank and traditional masculinity, but a feminine sensibility is reified through narrative throughout the series. Three episodes—"Frank's Return," "Frank Returns," and "Dueling Voodoo"—emphasize a particular version of Black feminine power through the characters of Miss Marie, a waitress, and Mme. Torchet and Ms. Tallent, both Voodoo practitioners.

In "Frank's Return," Frank, who has previously explained that he drove rather than flew to New Orleans from Boston because he is afraid of flying, shows his superstitious side. When he finds a gris-gris (a charm) in his father's desk drawer, he grimaces and hurriedly puts it back. Determined to ensure that Frank follows his destiny, Miss Marie, who had earlier visited the Voodoo doctor Mme. Torchet, explains to him that "she puts a spin on people." Frank laughs and replies, "Some more of your local color?" but then asks nervously, "What kind of spell did you put on me?" Miss Marie continues, quite seriously, "She put a spell on you so you wouldn't sell the restaurant to Pokie LaCarre." Frank is taken aback when he realizes that a half-hour earlier, when he had decided not to sell the restaurant, was the exact moment that Miss Marie was having a spin put on him. She tells Frank: "You can't go: you gotta stay." Anxiously, he asks, "What would happen if I left?" and Miss Marie replies, "I don't know—that would be the devil's work then."

This exchange between Frank and Miss Marie points to a conventional view of Voodoo as fundamentally evil and focused on causing harm to others. As this episode shows, however, Voodoo is more complicated than that simplistic and dismissive characterization. Miss Marie's intentions are benevolent: as soon as she meets Frank, she exclaims to the rest of the staff, who are distrustful of this Ivy League professor, that "he's a nice boy!" Later, she tells Hanna Griffin, who will become Frank's girlfriend, and her powerful wealthy mother Mrs. Bertha Griffin-Lamour, "He's a wonderful boy—really wonderful!"

It is surely not a coincidence that Miss Marie shares a first name with the most famous of Voodoo priestesses, Marie Laveau. Criticizing the appropriation of Voodoo by whites and tourists, Osbey explains that "the religion here in New Orleans is entirely within the sphere of women, whom we call Mothers" (4). Miss Marie, a kindly old woman, invokes Voodoo in other episodes, driving the plot—Voodoo spells actually do work—and reinforcing the association of a folk practice with the city.

Voodoo is presented in the series as an authentic working-class cultural practice, one that appears coterminous with traditional religious practice. As Miss Marie explains to Frank, "You gotta go to church here," and tells him that she is Baptist; other employees are Catholic, and Tiger, the bartender, goes to the Church of Divine Light and Daily Miracles, a Spiritual church. Spiritual churches in New Orleans, according to Claude F. Jacobs, were "organized by charismatic and highly individualistic women in New Orleans" and had an "openness to women ministers" and "an eclectic belief system" that included "voodoo" (314). The show's depiction of Voodoo fits Fandrich's description of it as "the common term in American English for any African-derived magical or religious beliefs and practices, often associated with . . . witchcraft" (779).

The second episode, "Frank Returns," expands on the effects of this feminine power. Frank had returned to Boston, but everything in his life has gone awry. He explains to the restaurant staff why he returned to New Orleans by detailing his bad luck in Boston. "Someone who watches PBS and drives a Volvo" like him did not believe in "a Voodoo curse," but "peculiar things began to happen" to him: "I had dreams, terrible dreams, the laundry lost all my shirts. My car was stolen, my telephone, any telephone I used would malfunction. The following week, the laundry lost everything, my girlfriend of three years told me she was leaving me . . . the toilet broke again . . . my office and classroom burned down." The powerful spell put on him by Miss Marie and the female Voodoo doctor brings him back to the restaurant. Frank decides to embrace his destiny, because, as he explains, "Since I left [New Orleans] my life has been a continuous nightmare."

The premise of the series, as Miss Marie explains, quoting the Voodoo doctor, is that "the son has to become the father"; this is an explicit statement of the role of surrogation. But this transformation is realized through feminine agency—through Miss Marie, a version of benevolent maternal power, and her female Voodoo doctor. The presentation of feminine power is one way that the show sets up New Orleans as real but different from the rest of the United States. The folkloric belief in spells is powerful and effective, and it has the secondary effect of making plausible Frank's move to New Orleans. As an outsider, he always asks for explanations of what is going on in the city, and his original dismissal of its belief and customs as "local color" makes their power and impact even stronger. Through the practice of Voodoo, Miss Marie reveals a version of an "authentic" New Orleans, showing that by participating in and respecting local practices, someone like Frank who has been raised up North can become a New Orleanian.

The fifteenth episode, "Dueling Voodoo," uses folklore to create a believable televisual sense of place. It presents not only alternative ways of knowing as feminine but also Frank's position as a pawn between two women wielding power. This episode builds on the pilot's portrayal of New Orleans as a site of feminine power through Voodoo. As mentioned, Frank has inherited rental property from his father. In one of his buildings, an older female tenant has driven all the other renters away with her strange and baleful behavior, and she has refused to pay rent since Frank's father died. This episode explores how Frank uses Voodoo to solve his problems with a destructive renter.

Frank goes with his lawyer Bubba to confront the tenant, but the wild and possessed woman easily intimidates the two men. Ms. Tallent (as she insists, the name is pronounced Tahl-aunt) has an apartment filled with dozens of birds in cages and a strange, spooky, and histrionic manner of speaking. She shares the surname (and its French pronunciation) of Robert Tallant, author of a best-selling sensationalized account of Voodoo in New Orleans; her crazed demeanor fits the exaggerated portrayal of Voodoo in his book. Ms. Tallent represents the antithesis of masculine repression and control; she has a different way of knowing and interacting with the world, as in Belenky's "women's ways of knowing." The dozens of cages filled with birds tweeting and chirping add to the pandemonium and witchery. As Ellen Moers and Maya Angelou have noted, caged birds often represent the feminine. With her long dreadlocks, scarf, and cowrie bead necklace, Ms. Tallent is a formidable sight, and her strangeness is heightened by the dim lighting in her apartment. With shots/counter shots moving from Frank's terrified expression to Ms. Tallent's grim determination, the camera angles reinforce her power. She remains regally seated as she explains to Frank why the other tenants have left: "They didn't show me any respect. So, they get headaches, their dogs run away, they have bad luck on their jobs." Eerie drums and bird hoots punctuate her words, accentuating her otherworldly power.

Ms. Tallent's version of feminine power utterly defeats legal mechanisms represented by the lawyer Bubba. When Bubba starts explaining the law to her, she starts screaming, "No lawyers" and "Lawyers out" with increasing volume until he leaves. Intimidated, Bubba refuses to confront her again, staying in the car when Frank later goes to serve an eviction notice. The weather turns rainy and blustery, and the notice flies away to land, mysteriously, on their car windshield. With his male lawyer proving not only ineffectual but also completely terrified, Frank turns to Miss Marie for consolation; Frank's position—sitting at a table with Miss Marie—makes his role as dependent, as needing feminine assistance, clear visually. She advises him to visit Mme. Torchet, the Voodoo doctor whose spell resulted in Frank's return to New Orleans.

The visuals for the Voodoo doctor contrast mightily with the horror movie sights of Ms. Tallent's apartment. The depiction of Mme. Torchet illustrates how the series presents stereotypical characters in non-stereotypical ways. She is very elegant, dressed in a pink sweater and black skirt, and wearing pearl earrings. With a tinkling harpsichord providing background music, she serves tea to Frank and Miss Marie in a porcelain tea set in a beautifully appointed living room. Miss Marie and Mme. Torchet sit side by side in chairs, looking at Frank, who is clearly in the role of supplicant to them. Mme. Torchet tries to reassure Frank that Ms. Tallent is probably just "some crazy old woman who's trying to scare people." Consoled and his fears minimized, Frank feels better and explains why he is worried: "I guess being in New Orleans and hearing about Voodoo . . ." She tells him, "Voodoo is mostly for tourists." So reassured, he asks whether Mme. Torchet's "spin" on him to run his father's restaurant is real. With hope in his voice, he inquires, "It will just wear off?" Intently, Mme. Torchet stares back at him, gently shaking her head. Her spin will not wear off, but Miss Marie advises Frank, "It's for the best." Without a visible token or charm, Frank's life has been directed by these two women. Instead of being angry or resisting, however, he accepts their interference, only asking that they help him evict the tenant who frightens him and who will neither pay rent nor vacate the apartment he owns. Lest Frank seem entirely selfish, the episode makes it clear that this tenant has also cursed the other people living in Frank's apartment building.

Mme. Torchet agrees to accompany Frank on his next visit to the frightening tenant, and as they approach the threshold, she becomes alarmed, saying, "I don't like this. I may have misread the situation." Yet, she slowly leads Frank up the front porch stairs, despite his nervously suggesting, "Maybe we should come back later." Mme. Torchet insists that they proceed and knocks on the door.

After they enter the apartment, the conflict between the two women and their Voodoo powers is vividly portrayed. Frank is tangential to the scene's dramatic action, serving only to hold Mme. Torchet's coat. His role is that of an observer to a fight, as his head follows the women as they speak, and he glances with trepidation at the bizarre behavior of the dozens of birds. He sits nervously to the side as the two women sit in armchairs facing each other and glowering. Frank sees some of Ms. Tallent's birds hanging upside down, a bizarre and unnatural sight. An uncaged owl swivels its head, staring at Frank. Anxiously, Frank says, "I got to go," but Mme. Torchet forbids him to do so by stating, "Not yet." Mme. Torchet and Ms. Tallent verbally spar as Mme. Torchet insists the apartment is Frank's property and Ms. Tallent retorts, "I own the soul of this place . . . he owns a piece of paper." Advocating for Frank, Mme. Torchet adopts the masculine legal perspective, while Tallent insists on a feminine, emotional view of possession of the apartment. Mme. Torchet concedes, telling Frank they must leave the apartment. Ms. Tallent wins this first female Voodoo contest, and a shaken Frank and Mme. Torchet depart (see figures 12 and 13).

Exiting Ms. Tallent's bird-infested lair, Frank and Mme. Torchet return to the Voodoo doctor's tidy domestic living room. Despite

FIGS. 12 AND 13. Ms. Tallent and Madame Torchet,
dueling Voodoo priestesses in *Frank's Place*.

the setback, Mme. Torchet remains calm and determined, plan-
ning the next step in her struggle with Ms. Tallent. She and Frank
discuss the situation, with Frank explaining that he was freaked out
when he saw the birds' bizarre behavior. Mme. Torchet says, "I'm
a Voodoo doctor and I'm telling you stuff like that doesn't happen." Frank replies, "I'm a college professor and I'm saying that it

does." This role reversal shows Frank's conversion to the Otherness of New Orleans folklore, as well as a destabilizing of stereotypes. While Mme. Torchet acts like a professor, consulting a book and doing research before deciding on next steps, Frank nervously asks her, "Aren't you going to kill a chicken?" She replies, "No, that's totally inappropriate," reminding Frank of her expertise: "I'm the doctor." Again, his stereotypical outsider's view of Voodoo practice is rebuked. He picks up Mme. Torchet's book (presumably of spells) but does not find an answer. He defers to her expertise, saying, "Just tell me what I should do."

He has already been feminized by his recourse to Voodoo to expel Ms. Tallent, and now this feminization is emphasized by his complete acceptance of an experience that is inexplicable in rational terms. Frank explicitly acknowledges Mme. Torchet's expertise and his need for her guidance. His anxious demeanor reveals that he realizes that he is out of his depth and has no skills or knowledge that will prove useful in this situation. A shaken Frank is converted by his experience with the two Voodoo practitioners: he believes the evidence of his senses, rather than common sense or rational thinking.

Unlike traditional doctors, Mme. Torchet makes house calls and, later in the episode, brings a Voodoo powder to Frank at the restaurant; he must put it on Ms. Tallent to get her to leave. He plaintively asks, "Can't we just make a little doll and stick pins in it?" She reassures him that the powder is the right spell, insisting, "It'll work—like a charm." She explains that not only must Frank apply the powder himself, because it is his property that has been put under a spell, but also Ms. Tallent must see Frank place the powder on her because Voodoo is "all in the head, Frank." Mme. Torchet epitomizes the professional, financially savvy Voodoo practitioner (the focus of Kodi Roberts's book, *Voodoo and Power*). She lives in a very nicely decorated home with color-coordinated furniture. She consults books before creating her spells and charms. And her services are not inexpensive. She charges Frank $400, a considerable sum of money in the late 1980s, and when he makes a face at the price, she challenges him: "You just try to get a powder any cheaper. I am practically giving it away." Later, we see Frank go to Ms. Tallent and, using a powder puff, apply the white powder on her face. Both she and Frank scream, and he runs out of the apartment. The episode ends with a male and a female uniformed police officer arriving at Frank's restaurant, saying they have received a complaint from Ms. Tallent. Frank's mouth opens, but no words of explanation emerge. Then the camera moves to Ms. Tallent, her boxes packed on the front porch, preparing to leave. She waves her arms in the air as she says she will "curse this house forever." The ending, in a manner typical of the series, leaves the outcome hanging. There is no tidy resolution of this Voodoo conflict.

These three episodes depict Voodoo as a living belief system that exerts effects not only on the locals but also on Frank, as he becomes part of the New Orleans community. Voodoo's feminine practitioners defeat the patriarchal legal system by operating according to a parallel but feminine-based logic. Placing powder on Ms. Tallent's nose reverses the blown-away eviction notice. Although the paperwork flew away and could be ignored by Ms. Tallent, the direct application of a powder is a form of eviction notice that she is compelled to respect.

Frank does evict Ms. Tallent, but to do so, he must seek the help of a female practitioner of Voodoo. By acknowledging and making successful use of feminine power, Frank has learned to navigate the city of New Orleans. The two Voodoo priestesses in "Dueling Voodoo" each enact versions of Marie Laveau, suggesting the ongoing influence of this feminine supernatural figure. *Frank's Place* evokes the trope of good and evil Voodoo in this episode, yet its overall characterization of the supernatural in the city is positive. Used by a grandmotherly, kind, and well-intentioned Miss Marie, Voodoo produces good outcomes for those placed under a "spin." The series depicts New Orleans as a place where people help each other by using traditional practices. Thus, it demonstrates how television can recuperate Voodoo from its negative associations that were generated in the nineteenth century by white enslavers who feared any source of power controlled by African Americans.

Marie Laveau and Voodoo Feminism

The Voodoo practiced by Mme. Torchet is an example of Voodoo feminism. Widely cited by scholars (Green 2012; Martin 2016; O'Reilly 2019), this concept reclaims the practice of Voodoo from its sensationalized depiction by writers such as Robert Tallant (1946). Noting that whites used Voodoo beliefs and practices to justify enslavement and their horrific treatment of Blacks, writers since Zora Neale Hurston have portrayed this religion as an empowering and positive force. That white men feared Voodoo and its challenge to their power is evident in the many laws prohibiting its practice (Long, *Laveau,* 94). Voodoo gave female practitioners and adherents alternative sources of influence and ways to resist and challenge white male supremacy. Given that its most powerful practitioners were female, Voodoo feminism acknowledges the practice as feminine and the power that it gave to women.

Depictions of Marie Laveau in folk stories, novels, and newspaper accounts emphasize not only her power but also her benevolent use of those powers. In *Frank's Place,* the Voodoo queen is never named, but Miss Marie's name and demeanor surely evoke Laveau at the end of her life, when she was praised for her healing powers and service to the community. Martha Ward's biography of Marie Laveau emphasizes her beneficence and the religion's fundamentally feminine nature: "New Orleans Voodoo, as the Laveaus [mother and daughter] practiced it, is one of many women's religions. . . . Women's religions are not set apart from the world's larger and better-known religions; they are an organic parallel, a female counterpart, a way to acknowledge women's experiences and losses" (99). In addition, Voodoo reflects W. E. B. DuBois's idea that African Americans living in a white supremacist society must hold a double consciousness—just as a skeptical

Yankee Frank must hold and embrace alternate views of a Voodoo reality. Voodoo allows Frank to see and eventually embrace an alternative worldview to white-male-dominated capitalism. As Ward describes it, Voodoo practitioners "see and understand things most people cannot. They exist in two realities, use two consciousnesses" (xvi).

Whereas *Frank's Place* offers a prominent mass-media representation of Voodoo, a novel can provide a deeper exploration through its innovative structure and insights into Marie Laveau's lived experience. The well-reviewed novel *Voodoo Dreams* (1993) uses journal entries, Voodoo signs (drawings that signify an integrative, nonlinear worldview), and first-person narrative to enable author Jewell Parker Rhodes to sympathetically portray the spiritual growth of a young girl into a powerful Voodoo queen. In contrast to accounts like Robert Tallant's nonfiction *Voodoo in New Orleans* (1946) and his novel about Laveau, *The Voodoo Queen* (1956), that sensationalize this historical figure, Rhodes depicts the travails of a Black woman living in an increasingly hostile, white supremacist society. Like "Dueling Voodoo," this novel explores conflicts between people trying to control Voodoo. In addition to showing how Voodoo offered hope to enslaved and free Blacks, Rhodes focuses on it as a spiritual practice that allows Laveau to throw off the control of white and Black men.

Marie Laveau's life is documented only sketchily in church archives and contemporaneous newspaper accounts, and many records from her lifetime are lost due to fire and other mishaps (see figure 14). It is a tribute to her power and influence that more than 140 years since she died, her name is still well known, and her purported grave site in New Orleans is still visited, with believers placing marks on the tomb.

In interviews, Rhodes acknowledges the difficulty of presenting an accurate portrayal of Laveau's cultural context, explaining that, in writing *Voodoo Dreams,* "there is a whole historical context that is needed in trying to deconstruct stereotypes about voodoo and then re-building and re-creating the sense of the African

FIG. 14. No portrait of Marie Laveau exists, but this image of a free woman of
color offers a view of her likely attire. Portrait by François Jacques Fleischbein.
Courtesy of the Historic New Orleans Collection, Acc. no. 1985.212.

past" (Quashie 438). To make her spiritual growth credible and
compelling, Rhodes focuses not on the gaps in the historical record, such as how many children she had and when and how her
first husband died, but instead on what it would have been like
for Laveau to grow up as a young girl in a world so hostile and potentially dangerous to her as a free Black girl-child. Rhodes does
not shy away from the mistreatment and sexual abuse that Laveau

faced, and her novel suggests how Voodoo could have offered the Voodoo queen and her followers hope and solace. Laveau "has to discover what strategies are available to her, which in part include gaining a sense of self, of her own self-knowledge, and within that, discovering her spiritual connection and the extent to which she has an incredible array of powers as a woman and spirit figure" (Quashie 432). In contrast to "Dueling Voodoo," which presents two adult women using Voodoo—one to harm and the other to help—*Voodoo Dreams* is a *bildungsroman,* the story of how a spiritual leader, as a Black woman, could gain such power.

Rhodes's portrayal of Laveau is "informed by thinking about how New Orleans as landscape and the whole sensuality that it suggests, the colors, textures and rhythm[s]" influenced her growth and development (Quashie 434). The novelist uses the liminality of New Orleans's geography to challenge Eurocentric perspectives. Young Marie grows up on a bayou outside New Orleans, spending her time outdoors and feeling free in the natural world. When as an adolescent her grandmère transports her to New Orleans in search of a husband, Laveau loses touch with nature. She then must rediscover it, first through a snake and her introduction to loas in the practice of Voodoo; later, when conducting Voodoo rituals, she gains the ability to walk on water. She creates charms from natural elements, such as dust and ingredients from animals and plants. She is at her most powerful, however, when she accesses and gives her body over to the divine. When that happens, she can perform miracles; while possessed she also takes the life of her evil partner John, who had betrayed her mother, grandmother, and herself.

Because Laveau did not leave a record of her life in her own words, Rhodes creates a white male journalist who, enamored of Laveau, writes an account of her experiences. Like Frank in "Dueling Voodoo," this journalist is a skeptic until he sees for himself the powerful effect the Voodoo queen Laveau has on other people. Laveau herself is dubious about the powers of Voodoo until she gains confidence and allows herself to embrace the needs of her followers, thereby gaining faith in a practice based on ancestral customs and connections to ancestors, which could help others. Rhodes identifies Laveau's conversion as a corrective to the horrors of a white supremacist, Eurocentric world. "Knowledge systems are different," Rhodes says, "We should value the different ways of understanding our world. There is something that none of us know about the world. Mysteries. Dreams. A world beyond" (Quashie 431). This knowledge is accessed through Voodoo, a practice that draws on the feminine and relies on female practitioners like Marie Laveau. In the novel, John—Dr. John in the tales about Laveau—resents the primary role she has in Voodoo, and he attempts to control her. Rhodes somewhat shockingly opens the novel with Laveau using her snake to kill John, allowing the rest of the narrative to enable readers to understand the existential threat that he posed not only to Laveau but also to the community of believers. By the end of the book, John's murder has been explained and justified. A more somber and drastic exercise of power than that in "Dueling Voodoo," his killing highlights the dangers facing women and vindicates their use of their powers to protect themselves and others.

Rhodes also emphasizes a key part of the Marie Laveau legend: that her daughter continued her Voodoo practice while pretending to be her mother after her mother's death. This interpretation helps explain some accounts of Marie Laveau's long life. The idea that a mother would pass her Voodoo knowledge on to her daughter, that it was a matrilineal tradition, is also key to its feminist character. Although Voodoo was African American in origin, white women also were drawn to it, as evidenced by the arrests made of white and Black women during one ritual held by Marie Laveau (Long, *Laveau,* 75). In her novel, Rhodes places Brigette, an unscrupulous and corrupt white woman, in Marie's path. Brigette, who is engaged in an incestuous relationship with Marie's brother Antoine, marries the journalist Louis who is chronicling Marie's life. Louis and Brigette's marriage, however, is not consummated, which creates a problem for Brigette when Antoine impregnates her. Humiliated by Antoine, who exposes her naked body to an enslaved woman, Brigette says out loud that had her father lived he would have protected her. But he is dead, and so Brigette seeks the help of Marie, who at first refuses to aid her; Marie then recognizes that "Brigette was a white version of her" (Rhodes 234). After Antoine attacks Brigette and Louis, Marie kills Antoine, protecting Brigette, Louis, and herself, as well as the enslaved people Antoine had abused.

Jewell Parker Rhodes's insightful novel has been praised for its portrayal of Marie Laveau as a believable historical figure and its depiction of the flourishing of Voodoo in New Orleans in the nineteenth century. The TV series *American Horror Story: Coven* (2013–2014) would bring Laveau into the twenty-first century, creating a version that would define her for a modern audience. The anthology horror television series filmed two seasons in New Orleans, one of which featured Laveau and Madame LaLaurie. Combining ironic and parodic humor with horror, this series exposes conflict between Black and white women by focusing on Marie Laveau and the infamous serial killer and torturer Madame Delphine LaLaurie. I agree with Tiya Miles's assessment that too many depictions of Madame LaLaurie conveniently present her as an aberration, rather than a product of the systemic and legally permissible abuse of the enslaved. But *Coven*'s portrayal allows Marie Laveau to exact a measure of justice by punishing LaLaurie, showcasing the supernatural as an alternative means to combat white supremacy.

The series *American Horror Story: Coven* won two Emmy Awards, was nominated for a Golden Globe, and enjoyed high ratings. Its portrayal of a struggle between a predominantly white coven of witches and African American Voodooists remains popular, and almost every New Orleans tour makes a stop at the purported homes of Madame Delphine LaLaurie and Marie Laveau. There is no evidence that the two interacted, but Ryan Murphy and Brad Falchuk's merging of their stories emphasizes Laveau as a warrior for social justice, resisting and challenging white supremacy. In this version, she is immortal and so can fight against racism for three hundred years, and even into the afterlife.

The evocative black-and-white title sequence depicts ominous figures, shown at oblique and disturbing angles. Many of these images are of robed and racially indistinct people. The close-ups, however, allude to Voodoo. Figures that appear to be white witches, demons, and devils are interspersed with visuals of the creation of a Voodoo doll and Voodoo symbols being drawn on floors. The viewers see figures sewing, but the material appears to be burlap, not cloth. Then in subsequent brief images, the doll takes shape, with the next image being of a Black woman's face no longer sewing but stabbing the doll. A few seconds later in an unusual color image, the woman sets the doll on fire and screams. Set next to these images is what appears to be a burning witch. The full meaning of the title sequence does not become clear until nearly the end of the series. Although none of the figures are recognizable as the characters in the show, the sequence depicts the conflict between witches and Voodoo; as it suggests, Laveau will set events in motion that lead to a witch being burned. The Voodoo queen's anger foreshadows her sabotage of the coven through a witch hunter whom she hires. Thus, this sequence sets up the theme of Black women's power and anger (see figure 15).

In its early episodes the series focuses on the white witches, as their numbers decline and their training school, Miss Robichaux's Academy, experiences setbacks. Run by Delia Foxx, the daughter of the order's Supreme leader, the witches' school evades detection by the public, while at the same time it is under siege by an organized and very wealthy group of witch hunters. Through historical flashbacks, viewers then are shown horribly graphic depictions of LaLaurie's torture of the enslaved. The series offers an alternative view of LaLaurie's later life. Although contemporary accounts assert that LaLaurie rode off in a carriage and escaped justice, in *Coven*'s version, Laveau is able to stop LaLaurie's abuse by taking advantage of her vanity. Laveau sells her a purported love potion that instead gives LaLaurie immortality. Leading a group of African Americans to the mansion, Laveau hangs LaLaurie's daughters just before she buries her alive in its courtyard. Laveau tells LaLau-

FIG. 15. Marie Laveau, as played by Angela Bassett
on *American Horror Story: Coven.*

rie, "What I gave to you was far worse. Life everlasting. . . . For your
sins you are damned to live forever. To never know the release of
sweet death. To never reunite with loved ones in the realm beyond
but instead, to be alone sealed up in your unmarked grave." Having
just seen appalling and brutal images of LaLaurie's torture and mu-
tilation of people in her attic, the viewer sees the justice in Laveau's
punishment ("Boy Parts").

Through more flashbacks, we see Laveau use Voodoo to wreak
justifiable vengeance on other murderous whites in the centuries
after she buries the still-living LaLaurie. In a sequence dated 1961,
one of Laveau's employees explains that she is sending her son to
a formerly segregated all-white high school. Laveau warns her that
it will be dangerous, but the young mother says, "I have faith in
the future." The sequence jumps to the young student on his bike
being pursued by three white men in a car, who brutally lynch him.
The next scene shows Laveau, with a stern expression on her face,
drawing symbols on the floor. Taking a snake, she slices it length-
wise, adding its blood to other ingredients in a fire. Bringing zom-

bies out from their graves, she sends them to kill the three men. Torn to pieces, they suffer as the Voodoo queen screams repeatedly to animate and direct the corpses to enact justice ("Fearful Pranks Ensue").

The series also highlights the inherent racism in the witches' coven, setting up the conflict between the two magical practices as racially inflected. In the second episode, "Boy Parts," Fiona Goode, the witches' Supreme (ruler), visits Laveau's hair salon. The historical Laveau reportedly worked as a hair stylist, thereby gaining valuable knowledge and connections from her clients. In the twenty-first century, Laveau continues to use her skills as a stylist as a cover for her Voodoo practice. The hair salon, Cornrow City, operates as a community center and place for Voodoo. As Laveau works in a desultory manner on Fiona's hair, they exchange bitter words about the ending of the truce between the witches and the Voodooists (brokered more than four decades earlier). Fiona has disentombed LaLaurie, keeping her captive in Robichaux's Academy. Losing her powers and facing death, Fiona wants the secret to immortality from Laveau. As they talk, Laveau works on Fiona's hair, but it is obvious that what Fiona wants is far more important than a beauty treatment. Fiona's traveling to the salon shows her desperation and need for Laveau's services.

In their verbal sparring, Laveau enlightens Fiona, showing the Supreme witch the racism in her false claims of superiority. When Fiona belittles Voodoo, Laveau exclaims, "Everything you got, you got from us." Denying the coven's racism, Fiona points to Tituba as one of the Salem witches who was part of the original coven. Laveau corrects Fiona's claim of racial inclusiveness, pointing out, "You made her [Tituba] a slave . . . she came from a great tribe—the Arawak. She learned the secrets of the other side from a two-thousand-year-old line of shamans . . . she gave it to your girls of Salem. A gift repaid with betrayal." As she enlightens Fiona, Laveau also enlightens viewers about Voodoo: "Maybe you haven't heard the news about civilization starting in Africa. We're more than just pins and dolls and seeing the future in chicken parts. You've been reading too many tourist guides." The camera angles and blocking reinforce Laveau's dominance over the witch in this exchange. A close-up of Laveau looming over Fiona emphasizes her vehemence and dominant physical position. Laveau reveals the Supreme to be an ignorant outsider, envious of Voodoo's power. Fiona sets a row of wigs on fire as she exits the shop because she has failed to obtain Laveau's secrets. As Fiona defiantly announces, "I want what you have, whatever it is that has kept you young all these years."

But Fiona's desire is never realized. Her emptiness is exposed when she invokes Papa Legba, a Voodoo deity, who agrees to give Fiona immortality in exchange for her soul. But as they are about to conclude the bargain, Papa Legba draws back, repulsed, announcing that Fiona has no soul to exchange. In the conflict between a white witch and a Black Voodoo queen, the queen triumphs (though Marie also eventually pays Papa Legba's price). *Coven,* then, gives primacy of place to Voodoo and Marie Laveau.

Laveau also recruits Queenie, a young Black woman in training to become an adept witch at Miss Robichaux's Academy, to work at her hair salon and to practice Voodoo. Queenie is a liminal figure, with both witch and Voodoo powers. Her decision to leave the witches' academy for the Voodoo shop is another defection that weakens the coven. Their numbers are so few, and Queenie's powers so formidable, that her loss is a grievous blow. Her surviving being shot by the witch hunter's silver bullet also demonstrates Queenie's superior abilities, showing once more that Voodoo offers more power than witchcraft alone. That Queenie comes to visit Laveau when she is making a gumbo reinforces the appeal of Voodoo. Participating in the culinary arts that draw on the senses and on African American culture contrasts strikingly with Queenie's past as a fast-food worker, a miserable drone in the maw of corporate food culture. Laveau offers Queenie real, authentic food that will feed her soul, as represented by the gumbo.

The ways that the white witches belong to a larger structure of white supremacy are also revealed by Laveau. When Queenie comes to see Laveau, the Voodoo queen enlightens her as she did

Fiona about the harms of white supremacy. As Queenie protests that witches do not care about race, Laveau corrects her: "They care plenty. Their power is built on the sweat of our backs." What Laveau offers Queenie is solidarity and the opportunity to live and work with people who share her experiences. "Every man, woman, and child in this house know what it feels like to be second best to some pretty little white girl. You come here and you never got to feel that again." A self-identified Voodoo doll, Queenie has the ability to harm others by harming herself, although she survives while her victims do not. Queenie is the only figure able to save Laveau from being killed by a witch hunter: thus, her recruitment saves Laveau's life. This example of Black female solidarity reinforces the message of antiracism and the importance of Black women working together.

Functioning as a center of employment and solace for Black women, Laveau's shop is depicted as a haven. In addition to helping Queenie, there are many instances of her affectionate and empowering treatment of Black women. She offers tender care to an older Black woman, Miss Cora, asking her, "Are you ready to be dazzled?" and reassuring her that she will be beautiful. Marie's delight is evident when she makes the older woman happy.

Although both Laveau and Fiona betray their daughters in search of magical power—Laveau giving her own child and infants every year thereafter to the evil Papa Legba, and Fiona emotionally abusing and abandoning Delia—the series's conclusion makes it clear that Laveau has a soul while Fiona lacks one. Fiona's daughter describes Fiona, not Laveau, as the coven's biggest enemy. As the Supreme, Fiona is charged with taking care of all witches, a job she fails. At the end of the show, both Laveau and Fiona end up in hell, but whereas Fiona is in a personal hell, Laveau is still punishing white racists. While Papa Legba chortles cruelly, she tortures Madame LaLaurie and her daughter, just like they tortured the enslaved in the 1830s. Meanwhile, Fiona is trapped in a rural house with a physically abusive male partner, the ghost of the serial killer, the Axeman. Her punishment is personal, with no political angle.

Although the portrayal of Laveau emphasizes her social justice mission, *Coven*'s depiction of the Voodoo deity Papa Legba is neither nuanced nor positive. As Jennifer O'Reilly notes, he is a stock Satanic figure with a tattooed face, sporting a top hat with skulls. His dirty fingernails and cocaine snorting with Fiona suggest that Voodoo is a disgusting and depraved religion (O'Reilly 35). His evil ways make Laveau look more benevolent, but that he captures her soul at the end implies that essentially Voodoo is a corrupt and dangerous practice.

The supremely powerful figure of Papa Legba contrasts strikingly with the reformed and expanded Robichaux's Academy. Fiona's daughter Delia has assumed the role of the Supreme. Her decision to come out in the open as a witch, revealing the coven to the world as a model minority group, has resulted in an onslaught of new witch candidates. The eager young women lined up for admission are an ethnically and racially diverse group. In another sign of diversity, Queenie has returned to Robichaux's Academy to be one of two young woman in the powerful Witches' Council, advising Delia. So, ultimately, the white-dominated coven emerges as the victor in the struggle between Voodoo and witchcraft.

As powerful figures who commune with divine powers and who can create life-altering or destructive spells, Voodoo queens are forces to be reckoned with. Yet, the nature of Voodoo is such that creating a potion, or protecting or attacking a person, requires a sacrifice on the part of the queen. This price is best illustrated by Queenie, as her regal name suggests. Queenie herself states that she is "a human Voodoo doll." Potentially far more powerful than any of the witches at Robichaux's Academy, Queenie can harm or protect others only by harming herself. When an evil male witch hunter comes to kill Laveau at her shop, Queenie saves her and others by shooting herself, in the process killing the attacker but also harming her own body at the same time. Queenie "dies" but is resurrected, thereby also earning, in an extreme fashion, the title of "undead."

In exacting justice against Madame LaLaurie, Laveau condemns the woman who tortured the enslaved, including her lover, to eternal life. But Laveau must remain eternally alive as well, creating a hell for herself at the same time. This type of sacrifice echoes the legend of the historical Laveau, who is said to have placed three burning hot peppers in her mouth for twenty-four hours, praying to God that a young man be found innocent in a trial. As a result of her actions, none of the witnesses were able to testify against the man, the son of a prominent citizen. Her sacrifice resulted in his exoneration, but she had to pay a price in suffering. This notion of sacrifice in Voodoo may also explain the many accounts of the historical Laveau's acts of kindness to prisoners and her generosity in helping the infirm and the poor, especially at the end of her life. In doing good, she not only ensured that she would receive a proper Catholic burial but also that her acts would balance the tension between the divine and the human, the dead and the living.

The presence of Voodoo queens in other supernatural television shows and films reflects the ongoing fascination with and power of this practice, even in series that focus on vampires, such as *The Originals.* This show acknowledges the importance of Voodoo, though it blurs the distinction between Voodoo and witchcraft.

FIG. 16. Voodoo shop in the French Quarter, in a scene from *The Originals.*

FIG. 17. Voodoo ritual from the film *Interview with the Vampire.*

A witch tour guide who becomes a powerful threat to vampires walks her tour group past the Voodoo shop featured in *The Originals* and advises them to enter while warning them of the supernatural dangers in the French Quarter (see figure 16). The shop's potions are effective, as the plot demonstrates, which supports the importance of Voodoo and its female queens.

A scene in the film adaptation of Anne Rice's *Interview with the Vampire* features a Voodoo ritual, conducted by the people enslaved on the vampire's plantation for the purpose of expelling his presence (see figure 17). Yet the vampire and his companions slaughter them all, heightening the evils of slavery, and the dominance— discussed in chapter 4—of the white vampire over Voodoo and ghosts. Even so, because the Voodoo practitioner correctly see the vampires as a deadly threat and perceives their danger when white people do not, the importance of Voodoo is reinforced.

That Voodoo still has an impact today can be seen in its many appearances around New Orleans in stores and varied settings (see figures 18 and 19). Consider the Voodoo queen tour that I participated in, which takes a serious, very respectful approach to Voodoo: it tells the story of Voodoo through Laveau's life and sites of

FIG. 18. An actual Voodoo shop. Photograph by the author.

FIG. 19. Voodoo Museum sign. Photograph by the author.

importance to her, including the place where her cottage stood on St. Ann Street (see figure 20). The guide, a young white man named Tim whose full-time job is teaching, talks about the historical records that document her life. The tour group members, mostly white and Black women, listen enthralled, despite the intense heat. Emphasizing Laveau's importance and ability to help

FIG. 20. Marie Laveau Apartments, near where her home stood.
Photograph by the author.

others, he also makes her something of a capitalist heroine, noting that she was an entrepreneur in monetizing her skills and performative abilities. Nevertheless, the guide disparages the touristy Voodoo shops, taking us instead to Voodoo Authentica.

Tim also cautions everyone about the dangers and costs of practicing Voodoo, telling the story in which Laveau placed excruciatingly painful hot peppers under her tongue. The harm of Voodoo to the practitioner is a constant in all narratives about the

FIG. 21. Krewe of Marie Laveau in the 2023 Sparta Parade.
Photograph by the author.

practice, especially the price experienced by anyone who would use Voodoo to harm others. Yet Tim also shows us that the place where Laveau once lived is considered sacred; many people leave tokens such as coins or hair pins to ask for her assistance.

Yet another very recent appearance of Marie Laveau took place during Carnival 2023, in the New Orleans Sparta parade on February 11 (see figure 21). In Carnival parades, walking organizations appear between floats, and these groups often promote serious causes (as in the case of the Amazons Benevolent Society, a group of breast cancer survivors and supporters; see Roberts 2019). Dozens of women followed a banner that read "Marie Laveaux, Voodoo Queen: Community Leader, Herbalist, Midwife, Healer of All People." Garbed in white, the women's swirling skirts and complicated tignons celebrated Marie Laveau as a model and icon. Carrying a painting of a Creole woman, the group acknowledged

Voodoo's history and presence in one of the city's most famous events, Carnival.

The wide range of representations of Marie Laveau, from *Frank's Place* to walking tours and even a Mardi Gras parade, are evidence of her fame and her power not only to entertain but also to generate respect and even fear. Because she left no account of herself, the historical woman remains mysterious. Even if we did have access to her own words, there is necessarily a divide between the real woman, the Voodoo queen as understood by those who believe, and the many different versions created by writers. Nevertheless, Laveau's grounding in New Orleans is central to her life and impact. By presenting an autonomous and self-sustaining Black New Orleans community, *Frank's Place* challenges traditional stereotypes of African American culture. *Voodoo Dreams* presents a glimpse of how a powerful woman like Laveau would have struggled and then exerted her power and influence. And although *American Horror Story: Coven* focuses on white female characters, it does present Marie Laveau as an important and powerful figure, both historically and today.

3

AMERICA'S MOST
HAUNTED CITY

x x x

I believe in ghosts now because
of New Orleans. I never did before.
I was so skeptical but now I've
seen one, which sounds
insane but it's true.

—BRETT DIER

Even famous people can be haunted by ghosts, particularly
if they buy a house that was the site of horrible torture and
a place from where the murderer escaped justice. Nicholas
Cage bought the infamous LaLaurie mansion in 2007. He thought
it would be the perfect place to write a horror novel. The horror
that ensued, however, was not of his creation. He never wrote the
planned novel, and even worse, Cage lost that house, and many
others, when he was forced to file for bankruptcy in 2009. Of the
mansion, he says, "You know, other people have beachfront property; I have ghost front property." While I never saw a ghost at
this property, I did see Cage there several times, as I was leaving
my own nearby apartment. Walking tours that stop at the LaLaurie mansion invariably mention the actor, even though he no longer owns the property, so my sightings of him now have the aura
of a spectral presence. Although Cage said he never experienced
the supernatural in that house—and he did not spend much time
there—his housekeeper, who maintained the home in his absence,
did. Instead of the screams of a young girl committing suicide by

FIG. 22. Real estate sign, promoting property as "haunted."
Photograph by the author.

leaping off the balcony, however, the housekeeper was plagued by innumerable ghost phone calls. Rather than being terrified, as a true New Orleanian she merely complained about the annoying interruptions to her work. Her account, however, indicates a feature of New Orleans real estate, especially that in the French Quarter, where properties are often advertised as "haunted" or "not haunted," with many buyers, like Cage, desiring a property that is haunted (see figure 22).

This chapter focuses on narratives of New Orleans's ghosts. Whether you believe ghosts are real or only fictional, these narratives provide vindication of their existence. First-person accounts are full of realistic and compelling details, and recent reports by "ghost hunters" provide evidence, such as unexplained lights and strange sounds, detected by specialized technology. Ghost stories, however, have a much deeper purpose than merely to scare the living. If ghosts are not "real" in a verifiable sense, they nevertheless manifest cultural anxieties and memories and have an important social function. From Jeanne deLavigne's literary retellings of folk stories to attempts to capture spirits on video, ghost stories share common elements. New Orleans ghosts want to be remembered or at least desire the justice of being remembered. Their suffering is usually connected to historical events featuring murder, mistreatment, and the perils of disease. In addition to tales presented as "real," fictions set in the city—such as *American Horror Story: Coven* and Victoria Schwab's novel, *Bridge of Souls*—depict ghosts shaped by history. Novelist Ariadne Blayde weaves her own experiences as a tour guide into *Ash Tuesday,* which features a ghost. For ghosts to have an impact, they must be believable in some fashion, and setting stories in the nation's "most haunted city," especially in the French Quarter, adds to their verisimilitude. Robert Tallant claims that "New Orleans has more ghosts than wrought iron balconies in the Vieux Carré" (*Gumbo Ya-Ya* 279), and the numerous ghost stories support this claim.

Although supernatural spirits can be said to be found in most cities, New Orleans celebrates its many accounts of gruesome murders and tragedies through the ghost stories it tells. A city of extreme contrasts of wealth and poverty that persist to this day, New Orleans exploited the enslaved and immigrants, especially the Italians and the Irish. The complicated provisions of the Code Noir, which allowed *some* people of color *some* limited rights as discussed in chapter 1, still generate injustice that defines and shapes the city's hauntings.

Examining New Orleans ghosts as they are recounted in folklore, ghost stories, novels, on television, and on numerous walking tours, this chapter focuses on what makes New Orleans's ghosts unique. Tales of spirits not only create a ghostly New Orleans but also provide evidence that the city is indeed a famously haunted place. To host ghosts, a place must have an environment conducive to spirits. Some of New Orleans's physical features are found elsewhere: its major port, large neighborhoods of historic homes and buildings, and periodic fog. But add to that New Orleans's role as a notorious site of slavery, its well-known pirates and battles, its beautiful but mysterious above-ground cemeteries, its recurrent pandemics, and its complex mix of cultures and spiritual beliefs about life after death. New Orleans's differences from other American cities and its being feminine and Caribbean or European, rather than American, in sensibility, contribute to the types of ghosts who dominate the city's narratives about itself. The female ghost haunting a beautiful home captures New Orleans's combination of beauty and threat.

In his introduction to *Ghost Stories of Old New Orleans,* noted folklorist Frank de Caro characterizes the appeal of narratives about spirits: "We like to experience the *frisson* of fear that comes from hearing such a story. Or the story gives us a feeling of connection to other worlds . . . [ghost tales] make haunting spirits more psychologically manageable, for many legends are about how a ghost is 'laid'—that is, how a ghost is made to go away, often by determining what has been troubling the spirit" (xv). Certain New Orleans ghosts help the visitor and resident alike reconcile the city's troubling, brutal past with its beauties and pleasures. If the ghost can be made to disappear, then symbolically the horrors it experienced can also be banished or at least put to the side. Ghosts help New Orleanians make peace with the city's past, and they also attract visitors, rather than scaring them away.

The stories of ghosts are kept alive by their retelling and by new sightings. People come to New Orleans seeking ghostly encounters, and by many accounts, they find them. Those who are less brave, however, can readily find New Orleans's ghosts in stories, film, and ghost tours. Ghosts generate more tourist activities than do Voodoo and vampires, perhaps because they are elusive and often less terrifying. Ghost tours have become the primary means by which ghost legends are told today (de Caro 3).

Disembodied creatures, ghosts remain on the Earth because they are trapped by the traumas of their lives and deaths. When their deaths are tragic—a result of disease, abuse, or war—these spirits remain in the place where they suffered. Some ghosts can be benign, as seen in an episode of *The Simpsons*, "Lisa Gets the Blues" (2018), which is discussed later. But most are malevolent—angry at the living and tormented by their misfortunes being forgotten. Murder, torture, emotional abuse, and abandonment motivate New Orleans's ghosts to inhabit the city with their presence as a form of protest. Even the stories of ghostly crossed lovers in New Orleans are clearly connected to the city's racial injustices, as this chapter will show. Unlike Voodoo priestesses and vampires, ghosts are not sought out by the living for their power. Yet, even though ghosts rarely intervene directly in the living world, their presence alone acts as a protest and reminder of injustice. Jeffrey Weinstock explains that ghosts offer "a form of cultural critique" (2), and sociologist Avery F. Gordon describes spirits as a representation of living people whom sociology and history have forgotten. Understanding the stories of ghosts in New Orleans provides insight into the city's history and its many tragic victims.

The names of haunting spirits are often lost to history. Even though ghost stories are based on once-living people, their surnames have evaporated, in part because the people who become haunts are those who were silenced during their lives: the enslaved, women, those who were murdered or lost their lives to violence.

Whether they are male or female—the most frightening New Orleans ghosts tend to be female—ghosts are by their very nature feminized. In contrast to vampires, who exhibit masculine traits including aggression, violence, and penetration (fangs), ghosts are liminal, shadowy, passive figures. They are less active than Voodoo priestesses, who offer an alternative to white supremacy and express the hope of affecting the living through rituals and spells. As emblems of repressed memories and history, ghosts function as reminders rather than actors. In addition, many ghosts (not just those in New Orleans) are the spirits of females who, having lacked a voice and power while they were alive, linger on to haunt until the injustices they experienced are corrected or at least acknowledged (for more about female ghosts, see Roberts, *Subversive Spirits*). The stories of female ghosts set in New Orleans reflect the city's unique reputation as a feminine, Caribbean/European city. New Orleans's stories are not about the stereotypical masculine characters that Horatio Alger made popular—poor white boys who become rich and successful. Instead, they are about lost fortunes, decaying mansions, and broken promises. Where the story of Marie Laveau presents a life of empowerment even in the context of legalized racial oppression, the tales of New Orleans's ghosts show another view of the feminine: ghost stories offer warnings about women's unfairly subordinate positions. That as a conquered Southern city New Orleans saw itself as unjustly dominated by the North before, during, and after the Civil War reinforces its feminine nature. Narratives of romanticized loss and of the violence and death caused by the misplaced love of women for men tell parallel stories of suffering. Because the suffering is in the past, listeners gain a sense of comfort about their own, less tragic lives. They can experience vicariously the dramatic and painful circumstances of others from a safe historical distance.

If the city's connection to Voodoo can be traced to one Voodoo priestess, its reputation as America's most haunted city can be tied to its high rates of death from disease, brutal conditions of enslavement, wars, poor sanitation, and natural disasters. That so many residents revere their ancestors and see them as actors in the world of the living encourages a belief in ghosts. New Orleans's above-ground burials in small house-like tombs provide a space where even today people readily can envision ghosts. Its spectacular eighteenth- and nineteenth-century architecture in the French Quarter and Garden District offers many settings perfect for ghosts. One hotel that served as a Civil War hospital is said to be haunted by the soldiers treated there, their screams from having limbs amputated without anesthesia still echoing in the halls. Another hotel was once a school that caught fire, and its students haunt the structure, playing tricks on guests and making noise running through its halls. Madame LaLaurie's French Quarter mansion still stands as an infamous monument to the torture and mass murder of the Black people she enslaved.

Almost every French Quarter walking tour takes tourists to the intersection of Governor Nicholls and Royal Street, frequently providing more entertainment than chills. Several tour groups often appear at the same time, each with its guide speaking loudly and gesturing dramatically, emphasizing performance rather than horror. One guide even uses a small hand-held projector to display a historical painting purportedly of Madame LaLaurie (see figure 23), preceded by a photograph of actress Kathy Bates as LaLaurie. Actually, no portrait of LaLaurie is known to exist. And the use of a television image to portray a historical crime illuminates the role of popular culture in keeping the supernatural alive in current memory. There is something inherently ghostly about using the image of an actress from a TV show to tell the story of one of the most famous haunted houses in the US. Yet fictional accounts of ghosts, like *American Horror Story: Coven* (discussed later in this chapter), are reinforced and corroborated by first-hand contemporary experiences with the mansion. Ghosts are the most plausible when they are based on actual historical events and are vouched for by people, most often female, who are alive.

Karen Jeffries, the initiated Voodoo priestess discussed briefly in the first chapter, experienced the ghost of Madame LaLaurie. The author Carolyn Morrow Long had invited Jeffries and two other "psychic women"—Mary Millan, a Voodoo practitioner, and Juliet Pazera—to stand on the sidewalk in front of LaLaurie's mansion on the exact spot where a crowd had gathered 174 years earlier, observing the brutal conditions that were exposed by a fire at her mansion (Long, *LaLaurie*, 180–184). After Millan performed

FIG. 23. Tour guide projecting a portrait identified as Delphine LaLaurie.
This is not actually Madame LaLaurie; no portrait of her
is known to exist. Photograph by the author.

a traditional ritual involving a bell, gourd, and smoke to open the
way for spirits to communicate, the three women felt the spirits
who had been trapped and had suffered in that house. All three
women felt physically ill after that experience.

Jeffries later had the opportunity to enter the mansion before
it was purchased at auction by its current owner. Although she felt
trepidation about returning to the place she knew was a site of extreme suffering, she also felt called to take advantage of such an unusual opportunity. For years, Jeffries had traveled across the South
with Southern Ghosts, a group that visits paranormal sites, investigating and documenting supernatural phenomena. One common

practice of ghost hunters is to ask any spirits they encounter to tell their story.

And so, after Jeffries entered the building, she went up to its second floor and mentally called Madame LaLaurie, telling her, "I would like to know your story." LaLaurie had a swift and angry response: "You can hear my story every night [referring to the large tour groups that stop outside the mansion nightly]. Get out, get out, get out!" Jeffries persisted; she had experienced many positive encounters with ghosts and was not easily deterred. So, Jeffries made another request: "Tell me about your slaves." This time the response was terrifying and ugly: "My slaves, my animals, my pets. GET OUT, you tawdry tart!" Jeffries ran downstairs, telling her companion, "I have to get out." Her friend insisted, however, that Jeffries instead enter another room where the enslaved may have been kept. Although the room was completely empty, Jeffries heard—as she had from the sidewalk—moaning and the sound of chains rattling. She asked the spirits, "Why are you here?" One replied, "We fell out of favor with Madame. She would bring us to the point of death and then back to life." Jeffries hoped she could encourage the spirits to cross over to the afterlife. She began envisioning the heavens opening. Knowing that the enslaved would have held both Voodoo and Catholic beliefs, she imagined African ancestors and loas, as well as Catholic saints, calling them up. Jeffries then imagined the spirits rising up. But she had left the door to this room open, and suddenly she felt Madame LaLaurie trying to stop these spirits from leaving. Angry at this evil act, Jeffries told LaLaurie, "You're not going to stop me," and continued envisioning freedom for the ghosts of the enslaved. When she sensed that all the ghosts had departed, Jeffries left the mansion.

Intervening in the world of the spirits comes at a price; like many mediums, Jeffries felt exhausted and had to sleep after spending time in the LaLaurie mansion. And that afternoon, there were five cancellations in the bed and breakfast she owned. Unable to even walk by the LaLaurie mansion without feeling ill, Jeffries sought out a cleansing by Bloody Mary, a psychic who runs tours and owns a spiritual shop. As part of the cleansing ritual, Bloody Mary lit a small cone of incense in a large glass ashtray. That ashtray, which was used often in her rituals, completely shattered as the cleansing ceremony took place. Fortunately, when a still-anxious Jeffries consulted Bloody Mary about the vengeful spirit of LaLaurie six months later, the reassurance came that LaLaurie considered Jeffries "insignificant," much to her relief. Whether the enslaved spirits were freed cannot be known, because the new owner of the mansion maintains it as a private residence. Yet the nightly tours continue to gather there on the sidewalks near the house.

Encounters with ghosts have been reported in diaries, newspaper accounts, and interviews. New Orleans's many nineteenth- and even twentieth-century newspapers, such as the *Times-Picayune* and more lurid publications *Delta* and *Crescent,* would cover ghost encounters. As recently as 2009, the *Times-Picayune* published accounts of ghosts in the French Quarter, and the newspaper invited readers to post their own ghostly encounters at its website (Fensterstock, 2). Robert Tallant, Lyle Saxon, and Edward Dreyer's *Gumbo Ya-Ya: A Collection of Louisiana Folktales*—published in 1945, the year before deLavigne's *Ghost Stories of Old New Orleans* appeared—contains many of the stories published by deLavigne, including one about the LaLaurie mansion. Tallant's accounts (he was the main writer) were obtained from hundreds of informants interviewed and documented by the Louisiana Writers Project during the New Deal. However, each story is very brief; many are only a page long, or even a brief paragraph. It is thanks to this federally funded project and deLavigne's book that we have such a rich lode of folktales specific to New Orleans. DeLavigne's lurid prose style is not for everyone; biographer and historical researcher Carolyn Morrow Long, for example, dismisses deLavigne as "adding disgusting details that are obviously the product of her perverted imagination" (*LaLaurie* 6). Yet deLavigne's details linger in current tours and other retellings, which suggests that the writing resonates and that it fills in what is missing from the historical record with vivid, graphic examples of evil.

That interest in New Orleans ghost stories continues is evident by the 2013 reprinting of *Ghost Stories of Old New Orleans*. If you ever take a walking tour of New Orleans, you will find yourself listening to many of deLavigne's versions of ghost stories. When folklorist de Caro interviewed a tour guide, she mentioned that she was familiar with *Ghost Stories of Old New Orleans* "and that her fellow guides had originally mined it for its wealth of ghost stories" (x). Although the city's walking tours include material on Voodoo and vampires, ghosts are their primary focus, as can be seen in their names: "Haunted History Tours," "Ghost Tours," "French Quarter Phantoms," and "Spooky Family Ghost Tour."

In addition to its well-researched source material and literary embellishments, deLavigne's book emphasizes the rich, florid, and unusual features of New Orleans's architecture, weather, and fauna. Not only the city's history but also its preserved buildings, especially in the French Quarter, offer a believable context for the presence of spirits. The Mississippi River can be counted on to produce early morning and evening fogs, the French Quarter's gas lamps produce an eerie pattern of dark and light, and the ornate ironwork balconies throw shadows and create a sense of traveling into the past. DeLavigne's "Author's Note" evokes the city's unique and palpable sense of otherness. I quote one of its paragraphs about New Orleans in its entirety: the vision evoked by these words now appears in fiction, television, and walking tours, but deLavigne should be given credit for an early characterization of the city's ghostly density:

> Every wall speaks of deeds that have transpired within its protecting confines—grim deeds, ghastly deeds, secret and sinister, most of them very long ago. The emotions, the tragedies, the terrible turns of an inscrutable and capricious wheel of fate—they storm and swarm anew in every winding staircase in the New Orleans French Quarter. Not a room but what has, at one time or another, sheltered some wraith. Some endured for a season, until their crying desire was appeased.

Some still walk, noiseless, unheeding, unseeing, pacing out their mysterious penance, night after night, year after year. (deLavigne xxi)

All the ghosts in deLavigne's accounts have full names, and many have addresses, adding to the sense that they actually existed. More than half of her narratives focus on female ghosts, whose femininity is central to their hauntings. Many of these stories emphasize their mistreatment, usually culminating in their murder by their male partners. At the same time, the stories reveal the economic precarity of these women, exonerating the ghosts from poor choices in lovers and instead reflecting on women's powerlessness. In "The Ghost of the Headless Woman," for example, a young woman named Alice Miner loves a young poet named Jeminy Crews. Alice also writes poetry, but because Jeminy has no financial prospects, she marries another man for his financial support. Worn out by the drudgery, both physical and emotional, of her life with her husband Charles, Alice writes verses and a passionate letter to Jeminy. When her husband discovers the letter, he grabs an axe and beats her head "to a pulp" (72). Charles is arrested for his wife's murder and executed. But Alice remains in the house, appearing to young women as a warning of men's brutality. Only in 1927, after a fire destroys the house where she was killed sixty years earlier, do the hauntings cease.

An abusive male partner appears in "The Ghost of the Treme Street Bridge," in which a young woman named Helen Rockworth is engaged to Jerome Gail. She then becomes involved in a scandal, and their engagement is broken. Jerome soon marries another woman. With no resources to support herself, Helen becomes a prostitute. Years later Jerome sees a destitute Helen with a baby, walking the streets. She begs him for assistance, but he spurns her, uttering curses. Distraught and with no resources, Helen commits suicide by jumping from the Treme Street bridge into the Old Basin waterway. Jerome and his wife are unable to have children, and they adopt a baby that he later discovers is Helen's child. Later,

Jerome's much-loved daughter tragically falls to her death from a window, and he commits suicide by jumping off the same bridge that Helen did. The spirit Helen continues to appear as a young, beautiful woman, as a haggard prostitute, and then as a fearsome hag. These various manifestations reflect the tragedies of her life, all caused by her fiancé's abandonment. "The Ghost of Love," "The Fountain Woman," and "The White Althea Tree" also detail the brutal mistreatment of women by their lovers or husbands.

The Civil War is in the background of all these stories, its social disruption a factor in these tragedies. The city's experiences during the war and afterward when it was under federal control reinforced its status as a conquered, subordinated, defeated city. In "The Ghost of the Headless Woman," Alice's lover Jeminy is killed in the war at the Battle of Appomattox. In "The Ghost of the Treme Street Bridge," Helen's fiancé was away serving in the war for four years, an absence contributing to her status as a fallen woman.

A warning about the dangers of trusting in fathers or father figures appears in "The Ghost of the German Countess" and "The Lady of the Door." Although the villains in the first story are pirates, the countess of the title—Frieda, the daughter of a wealthy ship captain—dies a horrible death because of her father's and her own misplaced devotion to wealth. Pirates, including the well-known Lafitte Brothers, are a distinctive feature of New Orleans history, and deLavigne's account locates this story's pirates in a house in Uptown New Orleans, then an isolated area of the city. After kidnapping Frieda and her father at sea, the pirates bring their captives to the pirate safe house. The daughter has hidden their assets in her gorgeous dresses, which she has embroidered herself to hide the jewels. When the captain refuses to reveal to their pirate captors where their wealth is hidden, both he and his daughter are tortured to death and their bodies hidden in a plantation house. The daughter returns to moan and wail in that house; her haunting ends only after the decrepit mansion is demolished and their bodies are found and given a decent burial. "The Lady of the Door" recounts the story of another beautiful, young, wealthy woman, whose grandfather locks her up in a hidden room to starve because she fell in love and refused to renounce a suitor whom he found unacceptable. Bernadine Lanzos, the young victim, takes her own life in an effort to exert control. Reflecting her need for acknowledgment, she haunts the mansion until, decades later, her body is discovered, and her story of injustice is told.

All these stories involve white men abusing white women; when the relationship involves a white man and an enslaved woman, the cruelty is even more brutal and the options for the woman much more limited. In "The Golden Brown Woman," a young octoroon—someone who has one Black great-grandparent—named Julie falls in love with the man who enslaved her. Although her surname is not provided, a specific location in the 700 block of Royal Street is given, a detail that presents the story as authentic. Julie's fate is described in chapter 1 of this book: after spending a December night on the roof of her enslaver's mansion, completely naked, she dies. Even today, she can be seen on cold winter nights. In deLavigne's words, the "phantom . . . walks, swaying and bending against the icy wind, teetering around the perilous corners, shivering in chilled misery . . . struggling and stumbling, hour after hour, night after night" (29). Since there was no justice for her death and her lover's cruelty, Julie appears as a spirit in cold weather. Her haunting evokes the brutality of those who enslaved Black people, as well as the capriciousness and evil committed by men against women.

In contrast to abolition narratives written by white women, many ghost tales emphasize the cruelty of white women who enslaved Black people. In "The Mystery of Madame Vaquer," for example, a white female lodger, Miss Abbie, abuses and kills an enslaved woman who works for her landlady, Madame Vaquer. The crimes are revealed only when Rosine, the murdered woman, haunts Vaquer. The landlady stands in for those white enablers who do not intervene in crimes against Black people. Even though a living enslaved woman, Sara, tells Vaquer of the evil committed by Miss Abbie, it requires an apparition for her to believe and respond to the crime. Vaquer investigates an enslaved woman's death only after Rosine's ghost gives her dreams of torture and even physical signs of abuse. She comes to understand the evils of enslavement and rejects it symbolically by throwing a hook used to abuse enslaved people into the Mississippi River. Abandoning her indifference and neglect of the enslaved, Vaquer takes action: she follows Miss Abbie and interrupts an evil ritual, causing the abuser to be killed by a snake. This tale suggests that some evil-doers cannot be punished by their deceased victims but require another living person to understand and expose the perfidy. At the same time, the ghost story also underlines the culpability of by-standers to racial injustice.

In the most notorious of haunted houses, the ghosts' terrible mistreatment was ignored while they were alive, and the perpetrators did not receive the punishment they deserved. After the fire in their mansion exposed their brutality, the LaLauries immediately leapt into their carriage through an assembled crowd on the streets and headed to Lake Pontchartrain; from there they fled to France, according to Long's archival research. DeLavigne states that Madame LaLaurie may have even returned to New Orleans fifteen years later, under another name. This part of the tale—that LaLaurie's ghost is still present in the city—is picked up later by *American Horror Story: Coven*.

Yet the enslaved victims of LaLaurie never received justice, and indeed their names were lost to history (until Carolyn Morrow Long's archival research recovered their details 170 years later). DeLavigne rectifies this absence by giving the murdered slaves names and personalities and focusing her tales on those unjustly killed.

"The Haunted House of Rue Royale" is the longest and most well-known story in deLavigne's collection. In describing the mysterious disappearances of the enslaved people in the LaLaurie mansion, she refers to them by name—"Where was Melanie? . . . Where was Carlo? . . . Where was Sara?"—and gives them specific attributes and skills. The young girl who hurtled to her death from the roof of the LaLaurie mansion is called Lia and is identified as Madame's personal maid. Lia is said to have angered Madame La-Laurie and ran upstairs to escape her brutal punishments. Running through the mansion's attic, Lia discovers other enslaved people held captive; they had been grotesquely and cruelly abused. Terrified by what she sees and realizing that she will be sent to this attic to be tortured, Lia jumps from the roof as the only way to escape a horrible fate worse than death. Months later, the torture chamber would be discovered when LaLaurie's enslaved cook, chained to the stove, in desperation starts a fire in the kitchen. Like Lia, the desperate woman risked death to expose LaLaurie's atrocities. Despite LaLaurie's protestations to leave the attic untouched, firemen broke into it to douse any flames that might have spread there—and to keep the fire from spreading to adjacent houses. DeLavigne first describes the hauntings of the tortured enslaved people and then repeats the graphic details included in a contemporary newspaper account. The authorial decision to describe decades of disturbing hauntings does more than heighten suspense; it also suggests that justice never was achieved. One of the worst female serial killers ever documented, Madame LaLaurie was condemned in a contemporary newspaper as "a Nero, a Caligula" (257). Six estimable gentlemen, including a judge, executed sworn statements attesting to her crimes. That the ghostly appearances were so numerous and consistent indicated the extreme nature of her offenses against nature. The "house," deLavigne explains, "began more and more to stand out as a weird and sinister menace to the community" (250) (see figure 24). It remained empty because of its "black wraiths [who] writhe and screech and rehearse over and over again some ghastly drama that had shunted them out of mortal existence" (252). Only after the Civil War did widespread poverty and the need for housing lead to the mansion being cleaned and refitted as a school for girls and then as a conservatory. With the arrival of Italian immigrants in the French Quarter at the end of the nineteenth century, it became a boardinghouse. But even these

FIG. 24. The infamous LaLaurie Mansion.
Photograph by the author.

people in desperate need of housing could not stay there because
of the ghosts. From the attic came "groans and wails and thumps
and a terrible rasping noise" (254), and the girl Lia was seen plung-
ing to her death, over and over again, presumably to avoid being
tortured by Madame LaLaurie.

Madame LaLaurie, as a female abuser, is an exception to the
pattern of male abusers; at least she is punished for her crimes in
American Horror Story: Coven. This television series, discussed
in the previous chapter, depicts Madame LaLaurie as kept alive

through Voodoo, but she is not the main ghost in the series. That honor belongs to the notorious Axeman, a documented serial killer in New Orleans who was never caught. An unsolved mystery about a serial killer, who identified himself as an invisible spirit, calls out for appropriation into other fiction set in New Orleans. At the beginning of *Coven*, the Axeman, who had been captured by the witches decades earlier, continued to be trapped in their Uptown New Orleans Robichaux's Academy (see figure 25). Freed by another student witch in the twenty-first century, his murderous powers are first put to the witches' service, when he helps them escape from pursuing witch hunters. After observing the coven's leader, its Supreme, for years, the Axeman falls in love with her and aids her in killing members of a witch-hunting society. The Axeman's plan is for the two of them to travel abroad, but she betrays him, preferring to keep her freedom.

The Axeman's appeal—he is a staple of many New Orleans–set fictions—is that he was never caught, and the motivations for his gruesome crimes were never fully explained. As his name suggests, he wielded an axe, hacking unsuspecting victims, usually while they were sleeping. He would chisel out a panel of a back door, break into the home, and then use a household's own axe to kill his

FIG. 25. The Axeman, as played by Danny Huston
on *American Horror Story: Coven.*

victim. As many as sixteen attacks from 1910 to 1919 were attributed to him, most committed against citizens of Italian descent. Despite the physicality of the attacks, the Axeman always escaped without anyone seeing him.

These bloody crimes terrified the city. Newspapers were full of speculation about the killer's motives and sanity. An open letter to the *Times-Picayune,* ostensibly from the Axeman himself, inflamed people's fears. In a grandiose style, he taunted the police: "They have never caught me and never will. They have never seen me, for I am invisible, even as the ether which surrounds your earth. I am not a human being, but a spirit." He continues with a threat—"I could be much worse if I wanted to"—and warns that he will visit New Orleans again on Tuesday night, but explaining that because of his fondness for jazz, "every person shall be spared in whose house a jazz band is in full swing . . . some of those persons who do not jazz it on Tuesday (if there be any) will get the ax" (qtd in Krist 291). Calling on jazz bands for protection in the city where the music was first created makes the Axeman a very specific New Orleans spirit. As Gary Krist describes it, the Axeman murders "remain one of the great unsolved mysteries in the serial killer literature" (332). Twenty-first-century accounts have shifted the focus from who the killer was historically to presenting him as a ghost. Given that deLavigne's anthology of ghost stories was first published in 1915, the Axeman's ghost story cannot be attributed to her. The book *Gumbo Ya-Ya* does contain several tales about the Axeman, but contemporary retellings have embellished them and reimagined him not as a deranged killer but as a ghost. In a way, depicting the murderer as a ghost feminizes him, weakening him from a brutal human to a wraith. Even as a ghost, however, he proves stronger than *American Horror Story: Coven*'s living witches.

The television series does not shirk from showing his bloody work; for example, a mutilated and bloody body in a bathtub appears in the scene where he seduces the witches' Supreme, Fiona Goode. The Axeman had been observing her since she was a girl at Robichaux's Academy, and he believes she is his soulmate. He does not kill Fiona, but her fate is much worse: she is condemned for eternity to live with him in his rustic country cottage, denied the urbane pleasures that she desperately wants to keep enjoying.

The series depicts the Axeman as an attractive white jazz musician; he plays the saxophone seductively and chooses his victims at the nightclubs where he performs. His saxophone case provides the perfect hiding place for his murderous axe, also suggesting the parallel between jazz music and transgressive and dangerous behavior. As a jazz saxophonist, the Axeman would be a less respectable member of society, associated with sexual misconduct and disruptive behaviors outside middle-class mores.

The Axeman of 2013's *American Horror Story: Coven* also makes an appearance in Victoria Schwab's *Bridge of Souls* (2021). Although this novel is marketed as a young adult title, its representation of New Orleans through its ghosts is precise, historical, and sophisticated. A *New York Times* best-selling author, Schwab has done her research on New Orleans's supernatural inhabitants. Her protagonist, a young white girl named Cassidy Blake, accompanies her parents—television presenters and paranormal investigators—as they research and produce TV shows around the world. Her parents are "world-traveling, ghost-hunting paranormal investigators" (4), complete with an electromagnetic field (EMF) reader that detects fluctuations in paranormal activity. However, Cass's own brush with death has made her more aware of ghosts than her parents realize, and her visions are more powerful than the paranormal-detecting machinery. Unbeknownst to her parents, she is an "in-betweener" or a "Veil-Walker," able to see beyond the everyday world to its ghostly counterpart. As a result, she discovers a New Orleans deeper and more complex than the one her parents are filming.

Even as Cassidy's ghost-hunting parents shoot a television show about ghosts, she is the one who encounters real ghosts, coming to understand why they haunt. As she learns about the history of the city and the spirits' specific tragedies, Cassidy realizes that ghosts want most of all to be seen and heard. New Orleans ghosts who were in real life marginalized and excised from official histories crave recognition. In many instances, she offers them release and escape from their entrapment in the city. As a Veil-Walker, Cassidy has the responsibility of banishing ghosts back beyond the Veil, where they can escape their miserable shadowy existence among the living.

Cass's encounters with ghosts are informed by her parents' research into New Orleans history. Her father explains the city's supernatural features through its historical context. New Orleans was, he recounts, "'sold to the United States, scarred by slavery, consumed by fire, ravaged by flood, and rebuilt despite it all. . . . Did you know that the city has forty-two cemeteries and it's home to the longest bridge,'" he pontificates, until his wife "pats his arm and tells him to 'Save it for the show, darling'" (26). It is Cass's mother who brings up the story of the Axeman, scaring even Cass's ghostly friend, Jacob. The salient facts that the Axeman chopped people up and was never caught set the stage for all the other ghosts based on documented horrors in the city. Yet the city's beauty and vivacity are highlighted by the family's encounters with second line parades, the delicious food in the restaurants, and the quirky and unusual people they meet. While Cass can see ghosts, and she has the mission of banishing them back beyond the Veil, she enjoys the beauty of New Orleans's unique cemeteries when her parents film scenes in several of them; she says of spirits, "They're usually pretty peaceful . . . the ghosts in the Veil are tied to the place they *died,* and most people don't die *in* graveyards. . . . On the whole, they're quiet spaces" (103).

With their cameras rolling, Cass's father points out Marie Laveau's grave. The novel reinforces the belief in Voodoo when the Blakes's local guide, a Louisiana native of African American descent, Dr. Lucas Dumont, explains the seriousness of Voodoo: "Not to be trifled with. . . . It's a set of beliefs, a form of worship, a form of magic" (104–5). Cass's friend Lara, another Veil-Walker, assures her early in their New Orleans visit that Voodoo is "very real" (24), and the plot supports Lara and Dumont's view. Voodoo even provides a ritual that helps Cass escape from an Emissary of Death that tries to wrestle her into the Veil. Both *American Horror Story: Coven* and *Bridge of Souls* present Voodoo and ghosts as real and dangerous; yet vampires do not appear in the TV show, and Lara reassures Cass that, despite the many tourist shops, "Vampires are not real" (19). This characterization makes sense: ghosts are the vestiges of actual people, and Voodoo was not only practiced historically but also persists into the twenty-first century. This historical basis for both Voodoo and ghosts reinforces their plausibility and verisimilitude.

Perceptive not only about the Veil but also about present-day New Orleans, Cass astutely observes the city's ambience, noting,

> The air is like soup. . . . But the heat isn't the only thing I notice. A horse-drawn carriage rumbles past us. A hearse goes the other way. . . . This is the living, breathing version of New Orleans. . . . The streets have names like Bourbon and Royal . . . wrought-iron balconies run like ivy along the front of every building. It's a collision of color, and style, and sound. Cobblestones and concrete, twisting trees and Spanish moss. I have never been somewhere so full of contradictions. . . . It's not the kind of place you can capture in a photo. [The ghosts are] wanting to be seen and heard. (10–11)

Schwab's vivid evocation of New Orleans's richness and complexity makes the novel's ghostly narrative persuasive and compelling. At the same time, the author makes it clear that there are charlatans and pretenders who exploit the city's reputation. Cass's parents are open-minded investigators who listen carefully to local experts like Dumont. But one of the scenes they film is of a séance with a medium who uses tricks to deceive the participants. Alistair Blanc, whose last name means "white" in French, is the Master of Spirits at the fictional Hotel Kardec. He attempts to reassure Cass by saying, "Don't worry. The spirits cannot hurt you," a statement that Cass thinks is "a straight-up lie" (69). The Blakes decide to film a séance, but Cass's father is clear that séances are "a *spectacle of the supernatural*" (67), a performed encounter. Yet, possessed by an Emissary from the Veil that is pursuing Cass, the fraudulent medium Alistair Blanc is terrified by a real encounter with a ghost; because of his fear of actual spirits, he cancels all future séances.

The tension between authentic ghost encounters and those that are fake is central to this novel and to other representations of spirits in New Orleans. That this tension appears in fictional depictions of New Orleans ghosts underlies two key features of the city: its uniqueness and its inherent unreliability. Ghosts and shysters alike are drawn to a city where the unseen can be monetized. Inherent in ghostly New Orleans tales is the idea that such stories reveal the "real" New Orleans and that those who merely intend to profit from tales of the supernatural are not only corrupt and dangerous to themselves and others but also cowardly. In this regard, the bravery and altruism of real ghost hunters make them heroic figures, like the Voodoo queen Marie Laveau discussed in chapter 2. The false medium Alistair Blanc can never lay a ghost to rest because he fails to appreciate their suffering and the meaning of their hauntings. He stands as a warning to the reader who might also take ghosts as mere entertainment, when their purpose is much more serious.

A productive and disturbing place to experience ghosts is Muriel's, a French Quarter restaurant well known for its food. Like most of the sites in Schwab's novel and *Coven,* it is a real place that is still in use today. Muriel's is in a beautiful old brick building across the street from the St. Louis Cathedral and Jackson Square. Off to the right of the main dining area on the ground floor is a small room with chairs and tables; its purpose is to direct ghostly activity away from the other diners. To placate the spirits, one table is always left unused by dining patrons, though it is furnished with bread and wine: that table is reserved for the spirits (see figure 26). This side room is cordoned off by a red velvet rope, indicating that

FIG. 26. Muriel's Restaurant ghost sign.
Photograph by the author.

the space is not to be used by the living. Barely visible through a window and a gate, the claustrophobic corner can be seen from Royal Street. Most ghost tour groups and tourists taking carriage rides stop there, stare, and take photos of the spooky space. Séances have also been held in Muriel's richly appointed upstairs rooms. As Fensterstock explains, "Haunted sites in New Orleans are a popular business" (2), and Muriel's promotes its ghosts.

Formerly a private home, the beautiful structure housing Muriel's was built by Jean Baptiste Destrehan and inherited by his

son Jean Noël, who was in charge of the trials of the enslaved people who participated in the 1811 slave revolt. Not only were both
Destrehans made wealthy from the work of the people they enslaved but the son was also implicated in the cruel treatment of
the rebels. Their heads were cut off and placed on poles along the
road from the plantations north of the city all the way to the city
line. As Cass's father explains, "Like much in New Orleans [this
building is affected by] the shadow of slavery . . . the building first
raised on this plot of land was used to house slaves before they
were sold off" (49).

This building was partially destroyed in the 1788 fire that consumed much of the French Quarter. Pierre Antoine Jourdan, who
bought the ruins from Bernard de Marigny, renovated the mansion.
Jourdan later lost it in a poker game and committed suicide there.
His restless ghost appears as an orb of light, and it behaves de-
structively, throwing items around such as silverware and other objects. Three times in recent years, the courtyard has been the documented site of glasses being flung from the bar to one of its brick
walls (https://muriels.com/about/ghost/). Other wraiths are
also said to haunt the space, but they are unnamed—presumably
because they were enslaved Africans who were held there. A
woman's voice can be heard upstairs, indistinct and unattributed
(https://ghostcitytours.com/new-orleans/haunted-places/
muriels-restaurant/).

Bridge of Souls gives a very detailed description of Muriel's:
"The restaurant on the ground floor is huge. Green ivy drips from
the planters hung like chandeliers, and big round tables have been
draped in white linens. A dark wooden staircase leads up to a land-
ing" (43). Cass visits an upstairs séance room and describes its
compelling aura: "The séance room is bathed in red. It's like walking into a darkroom, that deep crimson light, *just* bright enough
to see by . . . this room is cluttered as an antique store. Pillows are
piled on old sofas and ornate chairs. . . . There's a sculpture of a
woman dancing. . . . Two old-fashioned women in elegant dresses
glance up from a painting in an ornate frame. Tinny music whis-

pers through a speaker somewhere out of sight, an eerie old-sounding song" (47). The cluttered room reflects the building's layers of spirits from different time periods.

In Schwab's novel, even though Cass finds the restaurant beautiful and its food rich and delicious, she soon realizes that "Muriel's doesn't belong to just one ghost. It belongs to several. Each with their own story" (55). Overwhelmed by the many tormented, unhappy spirits—Jourdan who committed suicide, those killed by the fire, the enslaved who were held in the space before being separated from family and friends forever—Cass uses her camera to focus on just one spirit at a time and explains her gifts to her parents: "Ever since the accident [where she almost drowned], I've been able to see and hear the other side. Sometimes I can feel it, too. But in Muriel's, I can *taste* it" (43–44).

Schwab's novel cites other ghost accounts from deLavigne's book, including those taking place at the Place D'Armes Hotel, once a school where children died from yellow fever and the site of yet another fire (fires were common in eighteenth-century New Orleans). Cass's experience in the city overwhelms her, especially after the sun sets: "New Orleans *is* a different city after dark," she thinks. "The worlds of the living and the dead feel like they're colliding around me" (36).

As she notes at the very beginning of her New Orleans trip, "I try not to think about what happens to spirits who become real enough to touch our world" (7). The Axeman, who boasted to the New Orleans newspaper that he was a spirit, offers a horrifying example. Cass first sees him in Jackson Square, "a ghost lean[ing] against a post nearby, his head bowed and his boot thumping with the music" (135); what scares her is "the hatchet resting on his shoulder" (136). Only after Cass confronts the Emissary who is tracking her, and then saves her friends Lara and Jacob from being killed, can they together banish the Axeman. In a conclusive victory, the two Veil-Walkers Cass and Lara and their ghostly friend Jacob use mirrors to show the Axeman his true self. "'See and know,'" Cass tells him, as all three together say, "'This is what you are'" (291). They find the thread that allows him to remain in the world, and Cass and Lara encourage Jacob to pull this connection to the living out of the Axeman's chest. The serial killer ghost then "fades and disappears" (293).

A classic example of laying a ghost to rest, this vignette demonstrates that solidarity and affection can banish even the most vile and threatening spirit. The three characters are in their early teens, suggesting that their transitional status makes them effective combatants and protectors of the living. Cass, the daughter of famous investigators (though they use the terms "inspectors") of the paranormal, does more than investigate: she destroys evil and protects the living. This plot sounds like that of the popular television show *Buffy the Vampire Slayer* or any number of superhero movies. But the difference is that the setting and history are authentic. In eliminating the Axeman, Cass is not merely destroying an imaginary villain; she is destroying an actual serial murderer. Exorcising him asserts the power of the feminine in the world of the supernatural. As a feminine city, New Orleans offers and requires the services of Veil-Walkers.

Numerous television shows feature contemporary ghost hunters who investigate mysterious hauntings. Drawn to New Orleans for its many tales of spirits, these investigators employ complicated gadgetry and use mechanical means to confirm or refute tales of hauntings. As Schwab depicts in her novel, paranormal investigators rely on local informants to supply them with places and instances of hauntings. The show *Ghost Hunters,* in its thirteenth season, has visited New Orleans many times. One representative episode, "French Quarter Phantoms," shows how the city's history, old buildings, and spooky night ambience combine to create a plausible haunting.

The paranormal investigators from The Atlantic Paranormal Society (TAPS) draw on humor at times, beginning with the credits, where a "Roto-Rooter" plumbing van is transformed into a mobile hi-tech traveling laboratory. The TAPS founders also insist that, unlike other paranormal investigators, they assume that reported hauntings are bogus. Their skepticism is what makes their discovery of a truly inexplicable experience more compelling. Also essential to the appeal of their show is that they travel to experience the phenomenon on site. A ghost haunting is their destination, and sometimes getting there is another obstacle that they face. By depicting their journeys, however, the show emphasizes that the places where ghosts can be found are special. New Orleans's food and other tourist attractions are shown as motivating factors in the team's decision to take on a case in New Orleans.

In "French Quarter Phantoms," the TAPS team is called in to investigate a haunting in the Old U.S. Mint, now the New Orleans Jazz Museum. This building has also served as an armory and a jail. As outsiders, the TAPS members need to have local history explained to them. In this case, the Civil War provides the context for the ghosts. Built in 1835, the structure was taken over by the Union Army when it occupied the city in the 1860s. A Confederate sympathizer by the name of William Mumford objected when the Confederate flag was removed and replaced by the Union flag. In the dark of night, he removed the Union flag and replaced it with the Confederate flag, a crime for which he forfeited his life. He was hung on the front lawn of the Old Mint in 1862.

The hauntings that the director of the Jazz Museum, Sam Rykels, details to the TAPS cameras are corroborated by the security guard, Jimmy. Explaining that he is a converted skeptic of spirits, the guard recounts numerous inexplicable sounds and movements of doors throughout the building. "I don't believe in this," Jimmy states, "but I've seen it." Sara-Elizabeth, a receptionist, supports his narrative by confirming that she has also seen ghostly apparitions. Mumford seems to be the most likely spirit, but because the Old Mint was also a jail during Prohibition in the 1920s and there are records of at least one person being killed by a coin-pressing machine, the TAPS investigators decide to keep an open mind about who might be haunting the building.

The paranormal investigators do their investigating at nighttime. In keeping with their quasi-scientific frame, the time is included in an establishing frame: 12:35 a.m., 1:22 a.m., and so on. Throughout the night, the crew records using a variety of equipment, hoping to capture evidence of what they saw and heard and maybe even something that the human eye missed. In addition to video and audio recorders, the team uses infrared sensors, a geophone that measures vibrations (such as those made by footsteps), an electromagnetic field sensor, and electromagnetic thermometers to measure cold spots (a sign of ghostly activity). Throughout each sequence (and before each commercial break), the physical setting is emphasized by eerie external shots of the building and the French Quarter's historic architecture.

Because they are using night cameras, the images are not in color: they are mostly black and white, or at their most vivid, there is a sepia-type effect (see figures 27 and 28). Speaking in hushed tones, the investigators describe the physical sensations of being chilled by an unexpected breeze. But their work is most compelling when a door opens unexpectedly or a strange light appears on a staircase. These visual effects cause both the on-camera investigators and the viewers to feel a sense of estrangement. New Orleans's unique historic architecture—in this case a building first constructed in 1835—enhances the sense of the uncanny. The building's additions, such as jail cells in the building's bowels that were long since abandoned, increase the power of its history and the emotions those jailed may have felt.

In a move that validates Cassidy Blake's and other mediums' interactions with ghosts, the investigators endeavor to strike up a relationship with the ghosts. Although the TAPS team uses many machines to try to capture a spirit's presence, it is their attempted conversations with ghosts that are most compelling. In keeping with the idea that ghosts want the injustices they suffered to be acknowledged, the investigators first ask if the ghost is present and then try to make an emotional connection. Unsuccessful in contacting the executed Mumford, the team tries to speak with his mother, who is said to haunt the Old U.S. Mint. "Mrs. Mumford, can you tell us about your son?" they ask. After hearing moaning

FIGS. 27 AND 28. Ghost hunters and mysterious lights
in the Old Mint Building in New Orleans, as seen on *Ghost Hunters*.

and footsteps, and seeing a shadow, they ask her, "Can you do
something more significant for us?" And then a knock is heard.
Other investigators elsewhere in the cavernous building call for
Mr. Mumford as they see a shadow. Although they get "chills" and
see a shadow, they cannot tell whether the figure is male or female.
At 1:54 A.M., they hear a woman moaning and crying, and then
a rustling sound. Attempting to make her appear more explicitly,
they call out, "Mrs. Mumford? We have some information about
your son." A light appears without any verifiable source on the wall
above them, and they hear shuffling sounds.

As day approaches, the crew packs up their equipment, rolling up an impressive array of electrical cords. All these devices are loaded into their vans and set up in their hotel rooms, where they scrutinize all the recordings. They play and replay video and listen carefully through headsets for any audio recordings of ghostly sounds. The TAPS team makes an unusual discovery in their material from the Old Mint, finding physical evidence of footsteps, a voice, and a door opening and shutting without any other explanation (like the wind). Despite the TAPS team's stated skeptical attitude, in New Orleans's French Quarter, they believe they have evidence of a spirit.

In line with the feminine character of the city and of so many of its hauntings, the team identifies the spirit as most likely being the mother of the executed Mumford. When the main investigator Jay identifies the sound on the recording as a woman's voice, this offers confirmation of the presence of a female spirit. Sam, the museum director, agrees that the recorded moaning sounds like a woman. Jay then praises the Old Mint, saying, "You've got an interesting place here. It's got a great past. . . . We'd like to come back." He reassures Sam that the ghost is benign and poses no threat to any staff. "They have nothing to fear," Jay proclaims. Sam notes another benefit of the investigation for the Old Mint employees: "They will be glad to find that they are not alone [in the Old Mint] . . . that activity, that phenomenon may be real and not just their imagination." This documentary-style television series offers the same reassurance and invitation to their viewers—come to New Orleans to experience an authentic paranormal site, but do not be fearful because New Orleans, in general, is a compelling but also unthreatening city of the undead.

A similar attitude prevails in the guided ghost tours offered by many tour companies. As mentioned, these tours rely heavily on deLavigne's book, recounting many of its tales; more recent stories are told in the same manner, offering horrific details but as if remote from contemporary tourists' experiences. Greater emphasis is placed on the events that led up to the hauntings, such as

Madame LaLaurie's abuse of enslaved people, than the apparitions themselves. Often the ghosts are made to seem less dangerous because they are young women or children who posed little threat to others when they were alive, and less so when they are liminal, hardly visible spirits.

I participated in many ghost tours offered by Haunted History, one of the oldest and much-imitated walking tour companies. In one tour, the guide tells us the story of Julie, described earlier in the book. Like many guides, he is theatrically trained and is able to make Julie appear before us through a dramatic recitation of her tale; he gestures toward the spot where the woman died. Creating sympathy for a female ghost whose only mistake was to trust the man she loved impresses on the listeners' minds the cruelty of racial segregation and of men toward women. The historicity of the story reinforces a sense of superiority in the listeners, who feel (wrongly) that in the twenty-first century such abuses could never happen.

A recent tour led by novelist Ariadne Blayde emphasized a similar theme when she guided the group of thirty-two tourists to the Riverwalk, a pedestrian path on the bank of the Mississippi River. At almost 10 p.m., the setting is dark and eerie, with the river's current creating large swells and sound effects that heighten the tale's impact. Ariadne explains that in the late nineteenth century, when New Orleans was well known as a site of sin and debauchery, a young minister and his wife moved to the city from Connecticut. The minister explained to his wife, whom Ariadne called Julie (like the woman who died for love on a rooftop), that he was called to redeem the sinners in the city. He felt he was needed more in New Orleans than in Connecticut. Reluctantly, she agreed to move South with him. But their happy marriage was soon destroyed when the minister's failure to convert any sinners to a clean Christian way of life made him so distraught that he fell prey to gambling, drinking, and prostitutes. Julie consulted Marie Laveau, the Voodoo priestess who, Ariadne explains, was well respected and a practitioner of a legitimate religion associated with

Catholicism. Laveau ground up a powder for Julie to put into her husband's food, explaining that it would cure him but also warning Julie to use only a very small pinch: too much of the cure could prove deadly. Julie made a gumbo, following Laveau's directions precisely. But when her husband failed to come home, Julie added more and more of the concoction the later he was, so that when he finally showed up, the gumbo was heavily doctored. As he began to experience terrible stomach pain, Julie confessed what she had done, and her husband repented of his evil ways. Julie explained to her dying husband that she did not want to live without him, so the two walked slowly up to the riverside. As they reaffirmed their love for each other, the husband lay down on the riverbank. He took out his knife, telling Julie that he would help her into the next world where they could start again together. As he slit her throat, however, he began to recover from his illness. The two were found together by the river, and the husband was tried and found guilty of his wife's murder. Since she had presumably tried to poison him, the man was only sentenced to a life of hard labor and not execution. Julie, though, still haunts the place where she died—walking up and down the riverbank and searching for her husband who was to die and follow her into the afterlife.

Once again, the narrative of feminine weakness, ineffective attempts to kill, and a trapped spirit evoke the femininity of the city. Julie is one of the many female ghosts associated with watery places, the river representing the journey of life that is interrupted for women who were abandoned both in life and in death. Although this ghostly tale does not appear in *Gumbo Ya-Ya* or *Ghost Stories of Old New Orleans,* it nevertheless repeats those books' ghostly themes.

Another ghost story I heard on a walking tour was an "as told to me" narrative. It concerns the only elementary school left in the French Quarter. An imposing old brick building constructed in 1932, it is located where a nineteenth-century theater and school for boys once stood. According to the tour guide, this edifice had also served as a much-needed and very large mortuary used to house the many victims of yellow fever. Our guide, a former schoolteacher, tells us that she knows someone who teaches in the school. This teacher informed her that two of her nonverbal students had interacted with ghosts in this building. Children, especially those with special needs, are said to be more aware of the supernatural. One year, as the weather warmed up, the teacher noticed these two students behaving strangely. The young boy began waving his hands, as though flicking away insects, and began speaking—not to the other students or the teacher but to an unseen presence. And the young girl told the teacher that she had new friends and would often smile, gesture, or speak to them. As the weather grew hotter, however, these interactions took a dark turn. The young boy began waving away invisible mosquitoes, which, as we know now, were the source of yellow fever; he also said his friends were turning "yellow" (as if they were jaundiced). The female student said she had chills, despite the hot weather. When the teacher asked if she wanted to see the school nurse, the student ominously replied, "Too late." Clearly, the guide explained, these students were communicating with some of the thousands who died of yellow fever, who were most likely children because they were more susceptible to being felled by the disease than adults.

This ghost story stresses the specific history of New Orleans. While contemporary listeners can feel reassured that yellow fever has been eradicated, it is a poignant reminder of the tragic loss of life at an earlier time. Like many ghost stories of New Orleans, this tale is not easily verified. Yet the Vieux Carré Commission land survey of the French Quarter notes that, in addition to a theater and a school, the land held "assorted other nineteenth-century buildings" (https://www.hnoc.org/vcs/property_info.php ?lot=22928-01). Like the St. Peter Street cemetery, located in the French Quarter but since forgotten, an impromptu mortuary may have been one use that its owner preferred not to mention. The lack of sufficient space for the devastatingly high number of dead bodies during the frequent yellow fever epidemics, however, is undisputed.

The tour guide often made jokes as she told her tragic tales, with groan-worthy puns to lighten the mood. For the yellow fever account, she stressed that because the disease attacks the liver, victims would need a healthy liver to ensure survival. Yet New Orleans, she joked, is a big drinking town. In her account of the woman murdered by her husband on the Riverwalk, Ariadne made stereotypical fun of men overreacting to a cold, explaining that the husband may have felt ill but that, as events showed, he was not at death's door. The guide's use of humor on a ghost tour offers a way to minimize the suffering of dead victims, providing comic relief for what is otherwise a grim subject.

Ariadne Blayde's recently published novel, *Ash Tuesday,* offers a unique perspective on hauntings in New Orleans. As a tour guide, she knows all the historic tales and relates them with relish. In her fiction, however, she turns to a contemporary haunting. Set in the world of French Quarter tourist guides, *Ash Tuesday* explores the range of belief in the supernatural among this group. In her account, the guides themselves are as complex and scary as the tales they tell. One man identifies as a vampire and has dental work done to create fangs to prove the depth of his commitment to vampirism. Other main characters include a woman who tells fortunes and a trans guide who truly sees ghosts. Spoiler alert: the novel's narrator is a ghost, a recently deceased colleague who lingers on, deciding at the end of the novel that she feels more a part of the city in her guise of a spirit, after her death. Connected to her friends by their calling to tell the city's history, the narrator explains, "As they age with this living, dying city, . . . as they tell stories of ghosts, I will tell stories of them. Three hundred years of history. And now I have become it" (291). This serious novel, with its angst and vivid evocation of the city, conveys New Orleans's appeal and why a ghost might choose to remain here.

New Orleans's ghostly power also has an impact on visitors, and sometimes even a life-changing effect. Even in a sitcom format, New Orleans and its ghosts offer advice that visitors do well to heed. Another contemporary ghostly retelling appears in an episode of *The Simpsons*. This show, like many others, finds rationales to send its characters to New Orleans to generate new plot twists and to draw on the city's storied and colorful past for narratives. In "Lisa Gets the Blues" (2018), the family's brilliant and musically gifted older daughter struggles with being ignored and not being treated fairly because she is a girl. Her situation is one that often appears in ghost tales, and this episode follows the pattern. Fortunately, Lisa does not die or become a ghost, but because she is more sensitive and artistic than the rest of her family, she does see a ghost in New Orleans who inspires her.

Back in Springfield, Lisa's music-school band director discourages her musical gifts and talent for improvisation. As she plays a dramatic riff, he tells her to leave the classroom so they can talk. Although he acknowledges Lisa's musical skill as a saxophonist, he tells her to give up music. "This world is filled with Lisa Simpsons," he explains, "bright, talented, and doomed to disappointment." Devastated by his advice and the dismal prospects for musicians in general, Lisa cries and goes home. Her mother encourages her to play for the family, but Lisa discovers she has "the yips," a psychological block where well-rehearsed skills suddenly become impossible for the practitioner to perform.

As the family head off on a trip to Florida, their plane is mysteriously detoured to New Orleans, where they decide to vacation instead. The episode sets up a striking contrast between her father's gluttonous appreciation of New Orleans food and Lisa's interest in the city's creative and musical heritage. While her father makes himself a spectacle of overindulgence at New Orleans's famous eateries, Lisa heads to the cemeteries, where she communes with the spirit of Louis Armstrong. Standing in front of a larger-than-life statue of Armstrong with a handkerchief in one hand and his trumpet in another, Lisa wishes out loud that Armstrong could talk. His ghost appears, gratified by her interest in jazz. Armstrong encourages Lisa to continue her musical career, and tells her, "You keep searching, Lisa darling. You can find anything you want in New Orleans" (see figure 29).

FIG. 29. The ghost of Louis Armstrong mentors Lisa Simpson.

Armstrong's final words are mysterious: "Father knows best." Since we have just seen Homer's excessive indulgence in New Orleans food—he eats more than fifty Creole dishes—the viewer is as surprised as Lisa. But it turns out that ghosts do know best. Pursuing his adult pleasure of alcohol consumption but also trying to take Lisa to hear local music, Homer takes Lisa to a bar, having supplied her with a fake ID. There they encounter the nephew of a jazz musician who knows who Lisa is: this man's uncle, Bleeding Gum Murphy, has sent him a photo of Lisa, explaining she is "the most promising musician he knew." Inviting Lisa on stage, the nephew gets her to begin playing with the bar band. The crowd goes wild as she jams with the band; Lisa's love of music and skilled playing have returned.

When Lisa returns to Springfield, she is an invigorated and inspired artist, thanks to her encounter with the ghost. And significantly, Armstrong follows her back to her boring middle American town, remaining a muse and inspiration for her as he praises her playing and laughs. Lisa's journey is one that any tourist, television viewer, or reader of New Orleans ghost stories can share. The spirit of Armstrong corrects the sexism of her music teacher, and the city of New Orleans offers her the opportunity to regain her creativity. Although the episode never directly addresses the racism that Armstrong endured as a Black musician in the mid-twentieth century, it is implied by his refusal to sing for Homer one of his hits, "It's a Wonderful World." Armstrong complains instead, "It's a horrible world."

Although lighthearted, this episode of *The Simpsons* does reflect the emphasis of New Orleans's ghosts on injustice. A feminized city, New Orleans has an appalling racial history that generates ghosts. Different forms of ghost narratives allow for disparate emphases; the ghost tour and a television sitcom can use the horrors that create ghosts to generate humor that offers a brief respite from historically documented atrocities. Reality television series like *Ghost Hunters* employ the apparatus not only of television but also of EMF and other high-tech devices to corroborate the existence of paranormal activity. Novels and dramatic series like *Bridge of Souls* and *American Horror Story: Coven* situate the ghost in a fictional plot that brings historic events closer to contemporary society. Yet the ghosts that appear in these various media have a folkloric source—experiences with the paranormal by people who told their stories, and the written versions of these ghosts that appear in the straightforward recounting funded by the Works Progress Administration in the 1930s that provides the material for *Gumbo Ya-Ya* and *Ghost Stories of Old New Orleans*. Ghosts require more narrative construction, for although Marie Laveau and Voodoo are documented in records both from the past and present, ghosts remain outside the archive. Yet despite their liminal, shadowy status, they are an important repository of knowledge and historical critique.

4

DRINKING BLOOD IN
THE BIG EASY

× × ×

Monstrous! Vampires who pretend
to be humans pretending
to be vampires.

—VAMPIRE LOUIS DE POINTE DU LAC

Walking around the French Quarter on my way home after sunset, I often see strangely attired individuals and groups. People come to New Orleans to costume year-round, not just for Mardi Gras. The city often hosts festivals that encourage attendees to wear unusual clothes, like the pirates who show up for the Parrothead convention. Every once in a while, however, I have to stop and stare at someone whose striking look commands attention. This evening, one pale young man with long dark hair and dramatic leather pants and jackets is walking through the Quarter like he owns it. Although I do not see him smile, I can easily imagine fangs in that lean, hungry-looking face. At least two other writers claim to have seen vampires here, and their compelling accounts will make you look twice at certain people in the city.

Marita Woywod Crandle, who recently wrote a book on New Orleans vampires and who also owns the Boutique du Vampyre in the French Quarter (see figure 30), traces her ancestry to Vlad Tepes, a fifteenth-century ruler of what later became Romania, on whom Bram Stoker based his character Dracula. So, it may not be surprising that she once entertained a visitor at her shop whom she strongly suspected of being a vampire. The man was not dressed

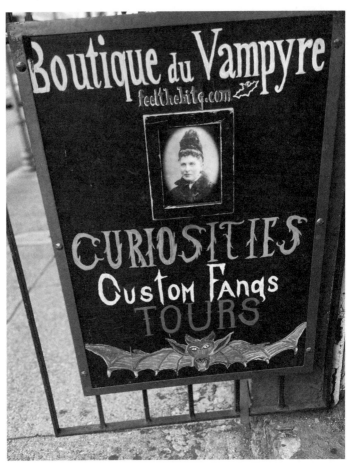

FIG. 30. Sign outside the Boutique du Vampyre.
Photograph by the author.

dramatically, as was the man I saw in the French Quarter one evening. But Crandle rightly points out that real vampires would not
draw attention to themselves by dressing the part. This visitor was
dressed elegantly, with a tailored suit and an impressive walking
stick with an ornate handle. Crandle's dog, otherwise a friendly
animal, took an instant dislike to him and growled. When the man
asked for a book on the history of vampires, Crandle felt nervous

having to explain that she only carried signed books in her shop. After browsing for a bit, the man left, just as Crandle's boyfriend arrived at the shop. She told him that she thought the man might have been a real vampire, but her boyfriend claimed not to have seen him, even though they must have crossed paths. In the vampire's mysterious ability to disappear, Crandle found confirmation of his supernatural nature. Fortunately, she said she never felt threatened by him, in contrast to another author who writes about the paranormal in New Orleans.

Kala Ambrose's encounter with a vampire was less positive. Whereas Crandle took the visit of a supernatural figure to her shop as a compliment, Ambrose felt her very life was in danger when she encountered a vampire. Ambrose is a "sensitive," a person who responds and can identify psychic energies. On a romantic carriage ride with her husband one night in the French Quarter, Ambrose felt a sudden chill, and the mule pulling their carriage inexplicably started bucking. The driver tried to keep the animal on course, but Ambrose countermanded his actions, telling the driver to let the mule change direction. Animals, it is well known, often react to the supernatural when humans are oblivious to it. As the carriage sped away in another direction, Ambrose saw a figure of a man and realized that the hypnotic threat had been coming from him. She recounted this experience to a paranormal researcher, Brad Steiger, who agreed that she had made a fortunate escape from a supernatural predator. Ambrose concludes this account with the statement that "vampires are not sparkly or friendly" (77).

Voodoo practitioners are real, historically documented people, and they perform rituals to the present day. Although ghosts have not been proven indisputably to exist, they can be traced to people who once lived. Vampires, by contrast, are widely acknowledged to be imaginary creatures. Even in fiction, vampires are discounted as merely myths. As the supernatural expert Lara reassures Cass Blake in the novel *Bridge of Souls*, "Vampires are not real" (19). And where humans have some control over Voodoo and ghostly interactions, with rituals and techniques designed to manipulate and even expel spirits, vampires often laugh at some of the ways people attempt to repel them, such as using crosses and holy water, as in Anne Rice's novels.

Vampires are different in other important ways from Voodoo practitioners and ghosts. Usually, vampires cannot abide the sun and so are confined to a shadowy, nighttime existence. Also, whereas Voodoo practitioners as exemplified by Marie Laveau are seen as sources of aid and information, and ghosts operate as warnings to the living, the vampire is a predator for whom humans are the prey. Vampires have mesmeric powers to sedate their human victims and to mentally control those who are not prey: they can confuse and distract and erase memories. They also make those humans whom they find worthy into fellow vampires. In this regard, the vampire undead differ from Voodoo queens, whose services someone might employ, or ghosts, who crave acknowledgment and justice.

Yet vampires share some features with Voodoo practitioners and ghosts. Like Voodoo practitioners, vampires have supernatural abilities that affect people. Like ghosts, vampires can appear and disappear, and even though vampires do have bodies, they are also gifted with superior strength and the ability to levitate and to transport themselves as effortlessly as ghosts. Sharing some features of Voodoo and some of spirits, vampires are stronger and more deadly than either Marie Laveau or any ghost—and less human as well.

Although there are female vampires, most are male. By drinking the blood of a human, they can transform that person into a vampire. The sexual implications, especially when a male vampire creates a new male vampire, are obvious. That the vampire is often an aesthete who delights in the arts and is pale, moody, and mysterious situates this figure within stereotypes of homosexuality. Even though male–male relationships between vampires and those between vampires and humans are not always overtly sexualized, they are characterized by a strong homoerotic attraction and tone.

The vampire is the consummate outsider, defying social mores, and is all the more compelling and attractive as a result.

Although Voodoo practitioners were taken to the Americas against their will and ghosts must haunt the place where they died, the vampire is more mobile—and in this, as in other features, markedly masculine. The vampire's very nature is predatory and aggressive; the most famous vampires are male; and their feeding practices invoke a male sexuality of coercion and assault. That their victims die reinforces the creature's masculinity, because murders in the United States, as elsewhere, are overwhelmingly committed by men (https://www.unodc.org/unodc/en/data-and-analysis/glo bal-study-on-homicide.html).

Many modern fictional works focus on the relationships between male vampires. Anne Rice's *Interview with the Vampire* (1976) and its film (1994) and TV adaptations (2022) are set in New Orleans. George R. R. Martin's novel, *Fevre Dream* (1982); the TV show *The Originals* (2013–2018); and the campy movie *Dracula 2000* also recount tales of male vampires in the city. These modern versions of the blood-imbibing undead can be traced to Bram Stoker's 1897 novel *Dracula,* yet its elements have been significantly revised. His vampire is an Old World European gentleman, but in the late twentieth and early twenty-first centuries, the vampire has moved to the New World. It is surely not a coincidence that, as his great-grandnephew Dacre Stoker attests, Bram Stoker visited New Orleans in January 1896, the year before he published his famous novel (Crandle 10).

Because of their unique qualities, vampires serve a function like real-world subcultures. Amy C. Wilkins, in a study of adolescent subcultures, notes their function for a socially isolated teen: "Finding goth also allowed him to transform the social pain of geekiness into an identity with social power" (33). Similarly, in the 2022 television adaptation of Rice's *Interview with the Vampire,* the title vampire Louis explains his motivation for becoming one of the undead. Louis, a well-off man of color in the early twentieth century, was an outsider despite his financial success. "You could be a lot of things in New Orleans, but a gay Negro man was not one of them," he explains in the episode "In the Throes." Vampire Lestat, who "converts" Louis, repeatedly points to the humiliations and restrictions Louis endures as a Black gay man and offers him the powers of a vampire as an alternative. It is with this offer of power, combined with the enticement of physical pleasures, that Lestat seduces Louis.

In *Vampire Legends in Contemporary American Culture: What Becomes a Legend Most,* William Patrick Day explores the meaning of these creatures. He finds that "vampire stories define a range of imaginative sensibilities in which ideas and thoughts are fused with a way of experiencing them" (169). The vampire, he argues, "brings a version of something we lack, a sense of the inexplicable and mysterious, of the possibility that not everything can be known and controlled" (169). In *Our Vampires, Ourselves,* critic Nina Auerbach explains that vampires "embody seditious urbanity" (7), an alternative to bustling, industrialist America that is focused on capitalism and materialism. What she notes about Anne Rice's vampires applies to the species generally: they are "a select club, a fraternity of beauty and death whose members are expected to be handsome and refined" (154). Both Day and Auerbach stress the reflective nature of vampires—ironically because of the standard trope that they cannot be seen in mirrors, their activities and interests are, Auerbach states, "personifications of their age" (3).

The city's natural but sometimes spooky beauty and storied legends have drawn writers and film and television show runners; there are vampire conventions, film festivals, a vampire boutique, and even a vampire-themed restaurant in the city. Crandle sees the allure of New Orleans as central to its vampire mystique: "I found shortly after moving to the Quarter, that people migrate to the city to become whoever it is they really want to be. Almost everyone has some level of curiosity about the vampire. That, combined with Anne Rice's popular vampires highlighting New Orleans as a vampire mecca, builds on visitors' curiosity" (19). The city's tolerance of alternative lifestyles contributes to its appeal for vampires, as well—at least from a positive perspective. Vampire victims, whether they are gendered male or female, are feminized in their relation to the seductive undead. As passive victims in thrall to a predator, humans—whether male, female, or gender fluid—appear in a feminized, subordinate position. As a feminine city, New Orleans, known for its charms and entertainments, offers an ideal site for vampires.

Urban settings also provide a darker attraction for vampires, as Steve Pile explains. In *Real Cities,* he examines the concept of "the vampiric city," concluding that "the city is the vampire's ideal home . . . [the implication is] that the city is itself vampiric—sucking the life-blood of its citizens" (97). He states that "one of the main cities attracting vampiric attention is New Orleans" (100), where a "vampire identity" can be created (100). Supernatural beings and manifestations are drawn to a place dominated by so much death—whether from fires, yellow fever, or violence—and by unique cemeteries and burial practices. "The vampires in New Orleans," he explains, "hide themselves in familiarity and [the] ubiquity of death" (118). Vampires' predation through blood evokes the blood mixing of slavery through rape, so that those who enslave share their heritage with those who are enslaved. Given that blood was mistakenly linked to ideas of race (which is a social construction, rather than a biological reality), the vampire serves as a symbol of predatory racism, raising "the spectre of race hatred" (122). But the vampire also exposes the falseness of human races, because "all humans are food" (122). That so many vampires end up in New Orleans, a major site of the enslaved's importation and exchange, is partly explained by this connection between blood and race.

A number of Dracula's descendants have chosen New Orleans from all the places in the world they could inhabit. Auerbach notes that "in Slavic folklore . . . vampires never ventured beyond their birthplace" (16). Yet in the last two centuries, the undead have wandered, with New Orleans becoming an important site of vampire stories. Vampires, like other travelers, seem to be drawn to

New Orleans for its seductive charms: its beauty, its mysterious landscape, and its acceptance of difference.

From its beginnings as a European colony, the Big Easy was an alluring residence for vampires. Just as with the city's ghosts, oft-repeated stories give credence to their presence in New Orleans. These tales draw on the city's history as a new home for those leaving Europe. Vampires are creatures with roots in a specific part of Europe. They derive, many say, from a cruel military prince, Vlad the Impaler, who lived in fifteenth-century Romania; he was also known as Vlad Dracula (son of Dracul). As his name suggests, he tortured his enemies. The great popularizer of vampires, Bram Stoker, borrowed Dracula's name from this historical personage, but the nineteenth-century fictional character was far more urbane and lived in the shadows, having to survive by drinking human blood. The secretive, clandestine nature of vampires and their need, as virtual immortals, to escape detection, made New Orleans a natural haven. Like other immigrants who made their way to New Orleans to transform their lives and find new opportunities, vampires found attractive its tolerance for difference and geographic and architectural features; its corruption and high rate of death from disease made it a sanctuary, enabling unexplained and violent deaths to be hidden more easily. As vampire Louis explains to the journalist interviewing him in AMC's TV adaptation of Anne Rice's novel: "It's New Orleans. Days are for sleeping off the previous evening's damage." The journalist Malloy nods, saying, "Perfect cover for a vampire" ("In the Throes").

Before the Civil War, the city was the largest site of slave trafficking in the country. As Walter Johnson explains in his book *Soul by Soul: Life in the Antebellum Slave Market,* "Thousands of slaves from all over the South passed through the New Orleans slave pens every year in the antebellum period, their purchase and sale linking the city both to the larger southern economy and the regional economy of the lower South" (7). As a key site of enslavement, New Orleans exhibited an indifference to human suffering that would allow vampires to practice their deadly eating habits.

Like New Orleans itself, the vampire is seductive but dangerous and deadly. The nineteenth-century transformation of the earlier monstrous, unthinking creatures into urbane gentlemen (and sometimes ladies) that Dracula epitomizes reveals the danger of falling for beauty. The city's natural beauty obscures the threats posed by its location—not just flooding but also the ready transmission of mosquito-borne disease and other ills among the people from all over the globe converging on this large port city. The magnificent architecture and sumptuous furnishings of the city were entrancing, but they hide their origins in the enslavement and brutal exploitation that made them possible. Even the city's lauded cemeteries, the "cities of the dead," cover up the fact that the elaborate tombs contained rotting corpses. The figure of the vampire, then, offers a perfect synecdoche of New Orleans. And as it does with so many of its attributes, New Orleans has made its vampiristic qualities part of its touristic appeal.

This endeavor has been aided by the many writers and film and television showrunners who have set their vampire tales in New Orleans, exploiting the city's vampire heritage. As Jeffrey Andrew notes, "In New Orleans, thanks to novelist Anne Rice's Vampire Chronicles sagas on the page and screen, it seems one can't throw a stone without hitting the undead" (Andrew 1). Spokeswoman for the New Orleans Metropolitan Convention and Visitors Bureau Mary Beth Romig cited the centrality of vampires to the city in the bureau's promotion of the Vampire Film Festival, an annual event that attracts thousands. The city hosted a second line funeral parade in Rice's honor in October 2022 (she died in 2021), and the 34th annual Anne Rice Vampire Ball was held as usual that same month (see figures 31 and 32). Halloween also draws many vampire enthusiasts to the city.

In New Orleans today, there are vampire "lifestylers," people who endeavor to live as vampires, even to the extent of having prosthetic fangs added to their mouths. John Edgar Browning defines a vampire community as one that focuses on its participants' desire to consume human or animal blood or psychic energy as

FIG. 31. Tribute to Anne Rice at the annual Vampire Ball.
Photograph by Suzanne C. Grim.

ways of strengthening themselves. Vampire lifestylers living outside New Orleans gather principally at vampire conventions and
communicate virtually, but those in the Crescent City are more
focused on local events and in-person gatherings. They participate in activities of celebration and fellowship, and the city "plays
host to some of the largest vampire events in the country" (6),
such as the Vampire Film Festival. Rather than seeing the vampire
groups as aberrant, Browning finds significance in their activities:
they manifest "'deviance' and self-empowerment" and may help
society "unfix the repressive and oppressive categories that lead to
marginalization" of groups of people (7).

One owner of a bed and breakfast has regular guests who
identify as vampires or as friends of vampires. She explains that
for most, the exchange of blood is symbolic, perhaps a few drops
from a pinprick. Other "vampires," though, have discernible cuts
on their wrists. One such guest recently objected to the inn's pol-

FIG. 32. Jason at the Anne Rice Vampire Ball.
Photograph by Suzanne C. Grim.

icy of allowing only registered guests on the property. She said she understood the policy but asked whether she could bring a male friend to sit in the courtyard. When told politely that would not be possible because the courtyard was still the lodging's property and covered by the insurance restrictions, the guest angrily asked, "Then where am I supposed to feed then?" Anyone interested in seeing groups of vampires in New Orleans will find they have their own bars, the Dungeon and Potions. Vampire "feeding," however, occurs in private settings.

Looking at these vampire texts from the 1970s to 2020s reveals certain constants—as Crandle points out, vampires are not sparkly and cuddly creatures—and some commonalities with Voodoo practitioners and ghosts. Like other supernatural creatures, vampires struggle with their powers and often want to use them in ways that might be positive. But because they are predators, they are hungry and greedy, and they need human blood to thrive: even the best of vampires represent the worst side of human nature.

In Rice's world, the Old World must and can be abandoned. Following Rice, other texts, such as George R. R. Martin's *Fevre Dream* and the film *Dracula 2000,* expand on the importance of New Orleans as an ideal place for vampires to thrive. As Lorna Piatti-Farnell explains, "The historical narratives of New Orleans become entangled with—and are, at times, almost inseparable from—the fictional chronicles of the vampire" (2). Yet, this connection between vampires and the city is a recent one; as Piatti-Farnell also notes, "Tourism pamphlets for the city do not make any mentions of vampire tourism before the 1990s" (3). The city's reputation not just as a site of Voodoo and ghosts but also of vampires is thus partly due to Anne Rice's influential *Interview with the Vampire* and its 1994 film adaptation.

A New Orleans resident, Kalila Katherina Smith retells the city's vampire legends in her 1998 book *Journey into Darkness;* she assures her readers that they are "backed by years of research and personal experience" (4). She explains the convergence of vampires in the city by pointing out that the city was founded by Europeans in the 1700s, when "massive vampire hunts were occurring" in the Old World (120). Today, "New Orleans is home to a subculture of beings who consider themselves to be vampires" (128), and she notes the influence of media culture: "Modern vampires have adapted the look of Hollywood" (131). But their updated looks still draw on historical murders and mysterious people who are identified as vampires. There are three principal vampire legends told on many walking tours and in novels, films, and TV series, all of which take place in the city's French Quarter.

The earliest tale is that of the Casket Girls, which is described in chapter 1. The struggling French colony in the early to mid-eighteenth century had a shortage of women, and so Bienville, its governor, wrote to the king of France, asking him to send marriage-able women to New Orleans. In some versions, the women were vampires in Paris; in others they turn into vampires during the long journey to New Orleans. Some accounts identify the women as of good family; others, more plausibly, suggest that the women, like the male colonists, were convicts or taken from asylums or the streets of Paris. All agree, however, that the women arrived with a dowry of sorts: clothes and other items stored in a wooden con-tainer, called a "casket" in French (according to Alcée Fortier, the term for "casket" in French referred to a small box holding valu-ables [Crandle 3]). Because the women were carrying caskets and many died on the journey by sea, the survivors came to be identi-fied as the undead in the twentieth century. Housing the women in the Ursuline Convent reinforced the idea that they were preda-tors and, to keep the city safe, had to be in a holy space. The time of their arrival varies from the early 1700s to 1751, when the nuns arrived. Arriving in the city from its earliest days, vampires can be said to have founded New Orleans, a claim that is propagated in fictional texts like *The Originals.*

As mentioned, most folklore vampires are male, and Dracula has a commanding manly presence, but the Casket Girls repre-sent an alternative, as befits the earliest vampire story of a feminine city. The female vampires, however, are described by Ambrose as choosing to hide themselves from society. This strategy can be explained by women's legal subordination in the eighteenth and nineteenth centuries. According to writer Kala Ambrose, the fe-male Casket Girls

> entered the world of New Orleans and created a powerful new lineage of vampires in the city, which reportedly re-mains to this day. While many vampire legends in New Or-leans focus on the male vampire, it is said that this was done purposefully, as the women had worked hard to conceal their identities. Many were able to enter society as their beauty and

charm opened doors . . . They reportedly worked with voodoo priestesses and witches in the city and provided aid and
assistance to them and continued to do so to this day. (106)

Two other stories of vampirism retold by Smith also take
place in the French Quarter. A mansion on the corner of Royal
and Ursuline Streets is said to have been owned by a vampire who
masqueraded as a family member over multiple generations. His
resemblance to portraits of members of the St. Germain family,
his mysterious drinking habits, and his violent acts perpetrated in
his house all pointed to him being a French count from the eighteenth century. After a prostitute leapt off a balcony at this house
to escape him, the police were called. But they did not arrest him,
and he fled without leaving a trace. Another oft-repeated story is
about a young woman who escaped from a scene of bloody violence in an apartment in the French Quarter in 1932. Two men,
the Carter brothers, had been holding many young women captive, tying them to chairs and bleeding them, presumably to drink
their blood. The police reportedly found twenty bodies, drained of
blood, at this murder scene. This story appears on the menu at the
Vampire Café, a restaurant whose staff all dress like vampires and
whose food and drink offerings are described and even appear to
be bloody. To her accounts of these vampires from the past, Smith
adds several contemporary encounters, including one of a young
man who worked with her as a tour guide for the Haunted History
tours. He became enamored of the vampire lifestyle, grew pale and
gaunt, and spoke frequently of St. Germain. Eventually he disappeared, after telling coworkers that St. Germain had asked him to
accompany him.

Anne Rice's 1976 novel *Interview with the Vampire* is undoubtedly the most famous vampire text set in New Orleans. Many crit-
ics identify Rice's novel as producing a sea change in the depiction
of vampires, evolving from the vampire as monster to the vampire
as protagonist (Day 43). According to Kathleen Rout, Anne Rice
was also "the first to show the moral ambivalence a fledgling vam-

pire might feel" (473). As this chapter makes clear, the city of New Orleans is integral to Louis's sophisticated and complex vampire persona. He is the owner of a beautiful plantation; its possibilities for secrecy and its ready source of victims in enslaved people who had fled to the swamps (as well as the enslaved themselves) draw the vampire Lestat to Louis. In the opening pages of the novel Louis explains to his interviewer: "The plantations . . . had a great deal to do with it, really, my becoming a vampire. . . . Our life there was both luxurious and primitive" (9). After his brother's death, Louis flees to the family townhouses in New Orleans, attempting to drown his guilt and sorrow in alcohol. He invites attack, careless of his own life, but rather than a brigand, it is the vampire Lestat who accosts him in the city. Louis spends many lyrical passages describing New Orleans as it was in 1791 when he transitions to vampirehood and to which he returns. What is so attractive about the city is its acceptance of difference: New Orleans offers not only the beauty that Louis hungers for but also safety. He describes its tremendous diversity of peoples and cultures:

> There was no city in America like New Orleans. It was filled not only with the French and Spanish of all classes . . . but later with immigrants of all kinds, the Irish and the German in particular . . . there were not only the black slaves, yet un-homogenized and fantastical in their different tribal garb and manners, but the great and growing class of the free people of color . . . who produced a magnificent and unique caste of craftsmen, artists, poets, and renowned feminine beauty. And then there were the Indians, who covered the levee on summer days selling herbs and crafted wares. And drifting through all, through this medley of languages and colors, were the people of the port, the sailors of the ships, who came in great waves to spend their money in the cabarets, to buy for the night the beautiful women . . . to dine on the best of Spanish and French cooking. . . . This was New Orleans, a magical and magnificent place to live. In which a vampire, richly

dressed and gracefully walking through the pools of light of one gas lamp after another might attract no more notice in the evening than hundreds of other exotic creatures. (39–40)

While Louis—and Lestat—value the cover the city offers their kind, Louis is also compelled by the city's beauty and its life. It is this vivacity that lingers today and continues to attract people.

Yet New Orleans's beauty and wealth are based on slavery, and particularly on the production of indigo and sugar—the latter offering, as Louis notes, a perfect analogy for the city's identity: "This refined sugar is a poison. It was like the essence of life in New Orleans, so sweet that it can be fatal, so richly enticing that all other values are forgotten" (41). In contrast to Lestat, Louis acknowledges the exploitation of the enslaved and feels guilty for drinking the blood of people on the plantation he owns. Yet, as an enslaver, he exploited and killed those who were enslaved even before he became a vampire. Claudia, a vampire companion to Louis, points out to him that he too is enslaved to Lestat whom, she claims, killed his maker and "would no more be a slave than I would be a slave . . . and you've been his slave" (112). He and Lestat also consort with prostitutes, doomed by venereal disease and social marginalization; as a vampire, Lestat's killing of these women is an extrapolation of the predation and exploitation they already experience from human men.

The city's high death rates and lawlessness also contrast with other cities that Lestat and Louis visit. "Never in New Orleans had the kill to be disguised," Louis recalls. "The ravages of fever, plague, crime—these things competed with us always there, and outdid us" (155). Claudia becomes a vampire as a child after her mother dies of yellow fever. When Louis finds her, he is ravenous, and so he drinks the pathetic young girl's blood as her mother's corpse lies nearby. Against Louis's wishes, Lestat then converts her into a vampire by having her drink his vampire blood. Her education about death and Lestat's attempt to reconcile her to being a vampire are facilitated when he takes her to see the unburied mounds of bodies of yellow fever victims. "'This is death,' he told her, pointing to a decaying corpse of a woman, 'which we cannot suffer'" (91). In a city rampant with death, a vampire can feel justified, as Lestat instructs Claudia, that "'we must never hesitate to bring death, because it is how we live'" (91). Claudia gains the wisdom and strength to challenge Lestat when she visits a cemetery on the eve of All Saints Day, a holy day in which the living spruce up the graves of the dead. Louis explains to his interviewer this unique aspect of New Orleans culture, where iron benches are set for families so they can sit and visit the entombed dead, as well as care for the graves of loved ones. "It was a festival in New Orleans; a celebration of death, it might have seemed to tourists who didn't understand it, but it was a celebration of the life after" (100). Visiting the cemetery sharpens Claudia's regret at not having a family; she also realizes that she will physically remain a young girl vampire and will never become a woman.

Later Claudia tries to kill Lestat, drugging him with absinthe and laudanum and stabbing him with a knife; Louis protests but she ignores him. After Lestat appears dead, she badgers Louis into helping her dispose of the body by pointing out that the body must disappear or they will be found out as vampires. Claudia and Louis dump his body in the swamp. Convinced that they will find vampires who will help them understand their vampirism, and who will be better companions than Lestat, Claudia persuades Louis that they should travel to central Europe to look for the original vampires. Although Louis agrees, he retains his New Orleans townhouse: he identifies as a New Orleans Creole who wants to see the roots of his European heritage, but he explains, "I was certain I would return sooner or later . . . and start a new life in New Orleans. I couldn't conceive of leaving it forever. Wouldn't" (135).

That New Orleans is the incubator of the vampire with a conscience is corroborated by what he and Claudia discover in central Europe and in Paris. The vampires in central Europe are mindless brutes—the beasts of vampire folklore, feared and hunted by villagers, and dispatched by them as the wild animals they are. They lack consciousness and language, sharing with Claudia and Louis only the insatiable hunger for blood. They are described as having "wagging, bovine heads . . . haggard shoulders . . . rotted, ragged clothing" (177). They resemble zombies rather than a sophisticated, articulate, and self-conscious vampire like Louis.

Although more evolved than their central European counterparts, the Parisian vampires are truly evil, without an awareness of the preciousness of life and having no ambivalence about killing wantonly, even when they do not need to feed. Louis finds himself drawn to one of the powerful vampires named Armand, who first betrays but then rescues him. But Armand has no pity for Claudia and another female vampire Louis has created for Claudia, Madeline—and condemns them both to death by being burned to ashes by the sun. The Paris vampires reflect their city, which is older and more corrupt than New Orleans. New Orleans's fragility separates it from its mother Paris, "so that New Orleans seemed at all times like a dream in the imagination of her striving populace, a dream held intact at every second by a tenacious, though unconscious, collective will" (186). Louis avenges Claudia's and Madeline's deaths by killing the entire clan of Paris vampires, except for Armand. In so doing, he demonstrates the physical and moral superiority of the New Orleanian vampires. He enacts justice because he cared so much for Claudia and was repulsed by the extreme cruelty the Paris vampires had shown not only to him but also in their twisted Théâtre des Vampires, described later in the chapter.

Eventually because of his love of New Orleans, Louis returns to the city. Despite traveling across the world and seeing its spectacular sites, he emphasizes, "I never forgot New Orleans" (290). He is bereft of emotion because of Claudia's death; only New Orleans could generate any feeling: "I would think of it acutely and I would feel for my home the only glimmer of desire I felt for anything" (290). And what Louis finds is a city that, though changed, also remains much the same. He experiences "the same sweetness and peace that I had known in the old day, not only in the dark, narrow streets of the Vieux Carré . . . it was a citadel of grace" (291).

He discovers "the town house where Lestat and Claudia and I had made our home, the facade little changed by fresh plaster. . . . Its two French windows still opened onto the small balconies over the shops below" (291). Louis realizes that Lestat, whom he and Claudia had not succeeded in killing, had also survived the massacre in Paris and that he is in New Orleans. As an indication of Louis's complete emancipation from Lestat and from the older vampire's materialism and lack of self-awareness, Louis confronts and rejects his maker. He rescues an infant who had been brought to Lestat to feed on, indicating that he is changing his ways. Although it seemed unlikely for an immortal, Louis recalls, "I was feeling almost that I would never leave New Orleans again" (299). He has come home, allying the vampire with his perfect setting. And while Louis has told his tale to the reporter as a cautionary tale, the young man is entranced by their interview and hurries off to find Lestat, presumably to become a vampire himself.

Although the 1994 film opens and closes with brief scenes set in San Francisco, Louis's life and experiences remain firmly centered in New Orleans. The pivotal encounter with Lestat—when he first embraces Louis and drinks his blood—occurs in a rough-and-tumble New Orleans that is beautifully rendered. Even though the tavern where Louis gambles and risks his life is made of rough-hewn wood and is dilapidated, the scenery, especially the backdrop of the Mississippi River and the port, is spectacular. A panoramic view of the river and one of the large sailing ships in port is revealed when Lestat flies up into the sky with a supine Louis in his arms. Dropping him into the river, Lestat baptizes Louis in a fashion, and the camera follows a sodden Louis emerging from the Mississippi River. His transformation and rebirth are just beginning.

In both the novel and the film, Paris is exposed as being jaded, cynical, and much crueler than the frontier city that is New Orleans in the late eighteenth century. The difference between the two cities is striking, and it shapes the character and behavior of the New World vampires, Louis and young Claudia, and the demonstrably evil Old World vampires of Paris.

FIG. 33. The play in New Orleans as shown in the movie
Interview with the Vampire.

New Orleans is rendered as a place of energy and art, brimming with life and death. As Louis stumbles away from the tavern with a prostitute, whose pimp will soon threaten him with a knife, we see scenes from a ribald play: it is performed on a rough stage in a nearby street. The play foreshadows that Louis will soon be reborn as a vampire. The Punch and Judy style performance by live actors wearing masks includes simulated sex and a birth scene. A male holds a woman in front of him, simulating rough sexual intercourse. The female groans and yells and then parts her skirts, from which a small male actor emerges as if in a birth. With much yelling and histrionics, a male actor pretends to throttle a female performer.

After Lestat turns Louis into a vampire, the two revisit the public house where another performance is taking place on a dark night. The two vampires sit at a distance, in the darkness under two trees. In between them sits a beautiful courtesan, whom Lestat first kisses and then attacks. Their placement in a natural setting reinforces the lesson that Lestat is imparting to Louis: to live, he must kill. It is a lesson that Louis resists, as he declares, "I will not take her life."

FIG. 34. The play in Paris as shown in the movie
Interview with the Vampire.

The New Orleans play identifies life-and-death struggles, presenting them as elemental. New Orleans may have muddy streets, yellow fever, poverty, and corruption, but it also demonstrates a dedication to the arts (see figure 33). A theatrical performance also figures in the scenes in Paris, but there the vampires themselves put on an elegant spectacle for a wealthy, invitation-only human audience (see figure 34).

The contrast between the crude and plain performance in New Orleans and the sophisticated spectacle in Paris illustrates the corrupting power of immortality. Although fancier and more erudite, the Paris play and vampires are infinitely more decadent and cruel. The time is the 1870s, when the rebuilt Paris is the center of European life, which allows even Claudia to note "how decadent" the city and especially its vampires are. And of course, while Claudia has not grown physically, her many experiences have made her more mature and self-aware. Before they attend the performance, Louis and Claudia revel in the city's beauty and arts, staying in a sumptuously appointed hotel and dancing to orchestral music. They are invited to the Théâtre des Vampires but are fearful of attending. The theater is large and is a cathedral-like setting, with a massive organ in the center of the stage. Louis is struck by the irony of the performance, which depicts "vampires who pretend to be humans pretending to be vampires." After brief vignettes where the objects of humor are a young couple and then a monk condemned to death, a young human woman is brought on stage. Terrified, she begs the audience for help. "I don't want to die," she implores. "Someone help me, please." The piteous young woman is toyed with by a vampire dressed in an elegant tuxedo. He pushes her around the stage, rips off her top, and then unbuttons and removes her chemise to expose her breasts. He taunts her with the fact that her beauty will fade, telling her she should not fear death because she will lose her beauty in life. Yet the woman still cries, "Let me live! I don't care." Armand, the oldest vampire of all and the troupe's leader, appears, seemingly coming to rescue her. But instead, he completely strips her naked, caresses her hair, and then forces her to face the theater audience. Picking her up, he raises her body before throwing her to a dozen or so vampires all cloaked in black, wearing hoods and crouching like hungry beasts. Appalled, Louis declares it "monstrous." Although he has killed many times in the hundred years since he was made a vampire, Louis still has a conscience and never toys with his victims as these Paris vampires do. The film emphasizes Louis's and Claudia's more humane behavior by not even showing them feeding until after displaying the extreme cruelty of the Paris vampires—and, even then, the New Orleans vampires only feed briefly. Claudia had imagined and done extensive research on Old World vampires, hoping to find guidance and knowledge. Instead, she and Louis find monsters who condemn Claudia to a painful and fiery death.

Armand, the dominant Paris vampire, is entranced by Louis and his emotions, describing him and Claudia as "two vampires from the New World, come to guide us into a new era." At four hundred years old, Armand is jaded, and he is struck by Louis's "suffering . . . [his] sympathy for the girl" they killed on stage. Armand tells Louis that he "reflects [this century's] broken heart . . .

you are beautiful, an immortal with a human soul." After the Paris vampires imprison Louis in a coffin, telling him he will lie there for all eternity, bricked up in their crypt, Armand rescues him. But Armand allows Claudia and the new vampire Madeline to be burned to a crisp. A distraught Louis finds their bodies and wreaks vengeance on the Paris coven, exacting the suffering they wielded on Claudia by burning all the vampires except Armand. A mind reader, Armand knew what Louis had planned but did not warn the others. In the church-like setting Louis is vengeance and death personified, wielding a scythe to kill any vampire who tries to escape the flames. In both the novel and the film, Louis appears as an avenging angel, delivering justice. Louis destroys the Old World vampires and, after traveling around the world to view famous artworks, returns to New Orleans.

Anne Rice reifies the notion of New Orleans as superior to Paris or any other place, because it represents a chance for a different life, even for a vampire. Much time has passed, and Louis marvels at the beginnings of American film, a technology that allows him to witness a sunrise for the first time in more than a hundred years. When he returns to New Orleans again in 1988, he says, "As soon as I smelled the air, I knew that I was home" (*Interview,* film). There Louis discovers his maker, a greatly diminished Lestat, huddled in a decrepit house near Lafayette Cemetery in the Garden District. Towering over Lestat as he quivers in his chair, Louis says, "I have to go," declaring his independence (*Interview,* film). New Orleans remains a sanctuary, a place of respite for Louis.

In *Interview with the Vampire,* Rice places vampires' powers above those of Voodoo and does not engage ghosts at all. On Louis's plantation, the enslaved workers and the Maroons (descendants of Africans who escaped slavery and lived in the swamps) realize he has become a demon. Yet their Voodoo ceremonies fail to repel Lestat and Louis, and the Black people all die. Although Louis feels guilty about killing a beautiful enslaved woman who is concerned about his well-being, he nevertheless drains her blood and that of all the others. A plantation owner, his vampirism symbolizes the predatory relationship of whites toward Native Americans, Africans, and African Americans and that of men to women in eighteenth-century New Orleans. The vampire is played by the alluring, sympathetic, and handsome Brad Pitt, reflecting the beautiful and enticing city that is also so very deadly. The novel and the film showcase New Orleans, its river and swamps, its wealth, and its beautiful buildings (see figure 35) and objects while always noting the cost of all this beauty suffered by enslaved people.

The recent adaptation of *Interview with the Vampire* as an AMC television series highlights the city's more recent role as a major site for media productions, especially those featuring the supernatural. In 2013, Louisiana (but mostly New Orleans) had the largest number of film and TV projects of any U.S. state ("Louisiana"), and in 2022, the film industry was projected to spend even more than the one billion dollars it spent in New Orleans in 2021 ("New Orleans Film Industry"). Trailers for the TV series were so complimentary about New Orleans that they could serve as tourist advertisements: they feature a horse and carriage in front of a beautiful French Quarter mansion; a recreated Storyville, the district of legal prostitution that enjoyed worldwide fame; and a street jug band of bass, banjo, violin, and washboard.

Dracula 2000 similarly draws on representations of contemporary New Orleans as a pivotal site for that most famous vampire. Directed by Patrick Lussier and written by Joel Soisson, the film is primarily set and filmed in New Orleans and highlights its culture as the draw for the supernatural creatures. The opening sequence of a sailing ship with all its crew killed by vampires appears in many vampire legends. In *Dracula 2000,* such a ship lands in London in the nineteenth century, but the film then jumps to the present day and moves the action to the Big Easy. The main vampire hunter, Abraham Van Helsing, draws his name from the doctor in Stoker's book. Although this character makes fun of Stoker, calling him a "mad Irish novelist," it turns out that Van Helsing is a little mad himself, having lived more than a hundred years. Van Helsing infuses himself with extracts of vampire blood to better combat his

FIG. 35. The Royal Street Mansion where Vampire St. Germaine lived, featured in the television series *Interview with the Vampire*. Photograph by the author.

nemesis, Dracula. In contrast to the evil vampire Dracula, Van Helsing never himself feeds on or kills humans. He has kept Dracula securely locked in a crypt in a high-tech London building that also houses his high-end antique store, as he continues to search for a way to kill him. Although in this version of the tale, ordinary vampires can be killed by a wooden stake, stabbed in the heart with silver, or shot by silver bullets, Dracula remains invincible.

The film criticizes the folly of materialist greed when a gang of robbers break into the antique store, but instead of stealing Van Helsing's closely guarded and immensely valuable antiques, the robbers take Dracula's body. Van Helsing's employee, Solina, masterminds the robbery, and Dracula rewards her with the death of her partners in crime. All the thieves become vampire food or vampires themselves. The robber Marcus is happy with his change in status; he comments that being a vampire is the only thing better than money.

After the vampire thieves load Dracula's coffin onto their plane (they are high-end burglars), they stupidly remove all the chains and guards that have kept Dracula trapped. The newly freed Dracula hijacks the plane and crashes it in a Louisiana swamp. Why Louisiana? Dracula is hunting Van Helsing's daughter who, because her father used vampire blood when he fathered her, has vampire visions. Since her mother has kept Mary ignorant of her father's unique occupation of vampire hunter, Mary has no explanation for her troubling dreams featuring a handsome but terrifying male figure (Dracula). Believing that Mary, the daughter, is his true soulmate, Dracula seeks to make her a vampire. By doing so, not only will he finally have female companionship of his own (diluted) blood, but he will also punish Van Helsing for keeping him locked up for so many years.

Mary's mother had earlier fled London for New Orleans, believing the distance from her father will keep the girl safe. But as events unfold, Dracula easily makes his way to the Big Easy, where he finds that its geography, hedonistic festivals, and religious beliefs make it a suitable place to thrive as a vampire. As Dracula walks through the French Quarter, he is handed cards promising him sexual delights, and he witnesses scenes in strip clubs and the drunken wantonness and scanty outfits of the female partiers. Of course, he has landed in New Orleans in the middle of Mardi Gras. The film graphically illustrates the extreme behavior of Carnival, with crowds chanting, "Show us your breasts," using drugs and alcohol to excess, and engaging in lascivious actions in the streets. People are in costume, everyone wears beads, and the overall impression is of New Orleans as depicted in the "Girls Gone Wild" videos.

While in New Orleans, Dracula converts three women to female vampires, in a nod to the events of Stoker's novel. As in that book, the female vampires are particularly disgusting. Their femininity is corrupted by their predatory fangs, their salacious seduction of those they kill, and their cruel behavior toward Mary, as well as their victims. Dracula's first female victim is a television news reporter who, while covering the plane crash, jokes with the cameraman about the appeal of her breasts. After she is turned into a vampire and is about to attack Simon, the protégé of Van Helsing, she taunts him, saying, "Haven't you always wanted to make it with a hot TV reporter?" Solina, the one who betrayed Van Helsing and is now a female vampire, similarly belittles Simon's masculinity before she tries to suck his blood; after she is committed to a mental hospital for acting like a vampire, Solina tells a psychiatrist examining her that she can see the doctor's penis through his pants. The third female vampire, Lucy Westerman (her name is another nod to Stoker's novel), is Mary's friend and roommate. Lucy endeavors to seduce Dracula, even though he has come to see Mary, and then brutally kills Van Helsing. Female vampires are depicted as disgusting nymphomaniacs, in contrast to the noble and tortured figure who is Dracula.

Unlike most other New Orleans vampires who have no relationship to organized religion, those in *Dracula 2000* fear Christianity. The most Catholic city in the United States, New Orleans offers refuge to Mary's mother, who fills her home with Catholic iconography. The city's numerous churches, seminaries, and other religious institutions are shown in the film. The first shot of the city focuses on St. Louis Cathedral; Mary always wears a simple cross around her neck; and several scenes take place in churches. She is friends with a priest, from whom she seeks help while giving confession. Even during Mardi Gras, New Orleans bears evidence of its religiosity—Mardi Gras, after all, is the farewell to the flesh and ends the day before Lent begins. Amidst the Mardi Gras crowds, there are usually mimes representing death, churches and crosses are in the background, and placards carried by fundamentalists very visibly offer alternatives to Mardi Gras. Their signs read, "Jesus Saves from Hell" and "Don't Destroy America with Your Lust." When Mary and Simon escape from the vampires, they realize they need to find a sacred place to be safe until the morning, so they go to a seminary that houses a library and a church.

Earlier in the film, Simon and Van Helsing try to figure out why, if Dracula is angered by holy water, the Bible, and any mention of Christianity, he is not repelled by them. He, however, can be trapped by silver and crosses; one of the robbers dismisses these artifacts as "all the voodoo." But the film supports the validity of Christianity at the end, revealing that Dracula is Judas Iscariot, who, for thirty pieces of silver, betrayed Jesus and then, distraught, tried to kill himself. In the film's version the rope Judas uses to hang himself breaks, and he is condemned to live forever with his guilt. This version of vampirism explains the lethality of silver: it represents the price of betraying Jesus. As Dracula watches Mardi Gras doubloons being thrown, there is an unexplained—until, that is, his identity is revealed—flashback of silver coins similarly falling to the ground. Even the characters' names evoke the Bible: Van Helsing's first name is Abraham, his daughter's name is Mary, and Simon is a reference to Simon Peter. In addition, Mary works at the Virgin Records store wearing a t-shirt emblazoned "Virgin." Since Mary is connected by blood to Dracula, she can understand what he has written in blood on the mirror in her hall.

The dramatic final battle occurs on a rooftop in the French Quarter that is not only decorated with wooden crosses but also dominated by a large, illuminated sign of a benevolent Jesus on the cross. With this backdrop, Dracula/Judas explains himself to Mary, whom he imagines will be his partner for all eternity, as a "vampire not bitten but born." Dracula tells her that God had used him because he needed Jesus to be betrayed, and now, he says to God, "I drink the blood of your children. You made the world in your image." Looking down on the wild revelry of the Mardi Gras crowds, Dracula cries out bitterly to God, "I give them what they crave most of all—the pleasure that you would deny them."

As Simon battles the remaining female vampires, killing them all after a vicious struggle with the conveniently handy wooden crosses, Mary tells Dracula that God still loves him. Dracula fights to dominate Mary, and they crash into the enormous image of Jesus. As it breaks, shattering glass, Mary grabs its electric cord and wraps it around Dracula's neck. They both fall off the rooftop, with Dracula holding Mary's hand. When Judas tried to kill himself two thousand years ago, the rope broke. But the twenty-first-century electric cord does not. Dracula lets go of Mary's hand, and she falls to the sidewalk in the now deserted street. But because she is still a vampire, she does not die. Dracula whispers, "I release you," and Mary's eyes turn blue, signaling her return to humanity. "This is how you die," Mary then tells Dracula, and as the sun rises, his body bursts into flame. His arms are spread in an echo of the Jesus statue above him, and though he suffers, this death is depicted as a release. Vampires were born in Jerusalem and lived in London, but it took New Orleans to end the species. Although this film seems to put an end to all vampires with Dracula's death, it also implies a future role for Mary, who has the film's final word: "I am Mary Van Helsing. I am my father's daughter."

A more recent production, set and filmed in New Orleans, makes an even larger claim for the centrality of vampires to the city. *The Originals* is a spin-off TV series from the young adult show, *The Vampire Diaries*. This show on the ABC channel focuses on a young female orphan and a love triangle—somewhat like the book and movie series *Twilight* by Stephenie Meyer. Taking characters from *The Vampire Diaries* and setting the series in New Orleans, however, makes *The Originals* a more adult-focused narrative. Since the titular family, the Mikaelsons—vampires Elijah and Rebekah and their hybrid vampire-werewolf brother Klaus—are a thousand years old, the adult emphasis seems well warranted. Although New Orleans, founded in 1718, is one of the United States' oldest cities, to these vampires who are from the Old World, New Orleans is very much the New World, a place of opportunity and expansion. A key feature of the plot is that the city was founded by Klaus in the eighteenth century, and he remained in New Orleans until 1919, a few years after Storyville, the legalized prostitution district, was shut down by the federal government. First Klaus and

Elijah and then Rebekah return to New Orleans in the twenty-first century to regain control of the city that they created.

The Originals claims more for the undead than other vampire texts, asserting that New Orleans is a vampire city because it was founded by Old World supernaturals. Beginning in 1713, the series gives its family of vampires a founding role in the city's development. Throughout the show's first season, all three vampires reflect on their arrival in New Orleans and their experiences in the city. They gain wealth and influence, even revealing themselves to an unnamed governor of Louisiana, who helps protect their secret. The current vampire king of the French Quarter, Marcel, whom Klaus made a vampire, acknowledges the Mikaelson vampire family's role in creating New Orleans, saying to Klaus, "Three hundred years ago you helped build a backwater colony into something." All three of the Originals have a somewhat feudal, proprietary attitude toward the city, reflected in their language of ownership and aspirations to power. Klaus, for instance, wants to be king of the French Quarter again, and Elijah recalls, "We did own the place and we were quite happy." Through flashbacks, the viewers see the dominant position of the Mikaelson siblings in the city throughout its existence. While Louis and his creator Lestat and young girl companion Claudia are at home in New Orleans, they hide in its background. The *Originals* vampires, in contrast, see the city as theirs, with human tourists as necessary for commerce and food. Humans, this series implies, are secondary in New Orleans to the supernatural community and its territorial struggles.

Having fled Europe, the Mikaelson siblings make New Orleans their home. Elijah defines their power in New Orleans as stemming from their "love and loyalty" for the city. He explains that the family "was happiest of all" in New Orleans. He, Rebekah, and Klaus returned to New Orleans because Klaus's miracle baby is being carried by Hayley, a werewolf, and Elijah plans for them "to build a home here together," which would include Hayley and the baby. While Klaus dismisses his brother Elijah's plans, telling him he "is a sentimental fool" in the first episode, "Always and Forever," the series reinforces Elijah's characterization as a leader and a humane, empathic vampire. Elijah promises to protect Hayley during and after her pregnancy and rescues a witch's body from the evil vampires so her sister can bury her. When the ruling New Orleans vampires oppress werewolves and witches, Elijah assures them, "I will fix this." He reminds his brother, who is more violent and less trusting, that "all we have ever wanted is a family." When Klaus taunts Elijah for what he sees as his weakness and sentimentality, Elijah replies, "But I have lasted this long in spite of it" ("Always and Forever"). Known as the ancient vampire who always wears a suit, he represents a vampire with a human soul. In contrast to Rice's vampires, who lose their humanity as they age, Elijah retains his optimism and commitment to relationships. His willingness to work with vampires and werewolves, and even on occasion humans, marks him as a supernatural mediator.

The Originals depicts New Orleans as a profoundly supernatural space, with witches and werewolves and vampires vying for territory. The vampires have triumphed, because the undead have powers that overcome those of witches and werewolves. Vampires can exercise mind control, erase memories, move with extraordinary speed, and kill with their tremendous strength. The Originals' power exceeds even that of ordinary vampires because they are truly immortal: they cannot be killed, though they can be put into hibernation through a silver dagger to the heart.

The exterior shots emphasize New Orleans's unique ambience; this series is set, like many others, primarily in the French Quarter. Numerous scenes are set on balconies, allowing not just for spectacular vampire leaps to the ground but also for a broad perspective of the city streets, an enhanced, superior view that would be appropriate for supernaturals (see figure 36). The packed cobblestone streets evoke a party atmosphere, while the historic architecture summons up an older, pre-technological world. Dimly lit by flickering gaslights, the streets are used to spooky effect as sites for

FIG. 36. Vampires on a French Quarter balcony with a view,
in a scene from *The Originals*.

murders and supernatural encounters. The cities of the dead are
also frequently used locations. Above-ground tombs and wrought-
iron cemetery fences with large trees dripping with Spanish moss
offer a believable backdrop for the vampires' powers (see figure
37). These are the spaces Elijah travels through as he attempts to
broker a deal to protect his family and the other supernaturals,
who are currently being oppressed and killed for violating the
edicts of Marcel, the king vampire.

The vampires' control of New Orleans is aided by the city's
raucous party culture, depicted repeatedly in long-shot views of
Bourbon Street. In "Always and Forever," a tour guide saunters
through the French Quarter, telling her group, "Welcome to New
Orleans and the crown jewel of the Crescent City, the French
Quarter. Jazz and jambalaya, romance and poetry, not to mention
the things that go bump in the night, monsters that feed off human
blood, vengeful spirits of the dead" ("Always and Forever"). The
tour guide's spiel is echoed later in the episode, when Marcel explains how vampires find their victims. "The city of New Orleans

FIG. 37. One of the many cemetery scenes in *The Originals*.

attracts people from all over the country," he explains. "They come here to party in our streets. Some are just looking for some fun, some are looking for something a little darker, more dangerous." The next scene shows a young couple being handed a poster that reads, "The Abattoir—where the party never ends." The couple go to Marcel's mansion and enjoy music, alcohol, and drugs, until the vampires begin leaping off the interior courtyard balcony to feast on the guests. Marcel describes it as "the occasional all-night buffet." Some guests die; others are restored with a little vampire blood and have their memories erased. Appropriately the vampires hold most of their meetings in bars—the French Quarter is reputed to have more bars than any other thirteen blocks in any other city. While Elijah sees vampires as a family, Marcel runs his organization like a fraternity, with adherents earning rings that allow them to endure daylight for services rendered to him.

The Originals' experiences in New Orleans, especially the flashbacks to earlier time periods, evoke the unique features of the city's history that align with vampirism and predation. The conflict between the brothers—Elijah the compassionate, who is reminiscent of Louis from *Interview with the Vampire,* and Klaus, the crueler and more brutal vampire/werewolf who recalls Lestat—dominates the series, but their sister vampire Rebekah brings to life a feminist version of the supernatural connected to New Orleans history. The legend of the Casket Girls, described in chapter 1, appears in numerous histories of the city, and is based on the importation of young women from France to serve as brides for the French colonists. But as Mary Gehman and Nancy Ries (2013) note in *Women and New Orleans,* there is no archival evidence for them.

That has not stopped these tales of eligible young women—arriving in New Orleans on a ship, escorted by nuns—from being turned into the stuff of vampire legends, as numerous books and walking tours repeat the story and attach it to a mysterious third floor of the Ursuline Convent. The allure of these tales stems partly from these young women's tragic lives and deaths; like so many involuntary immigrants, they survived a dangerous journey by sea, only to then suffer poor health. That so many young women died led to the notion that they came to New Orleans not while alive but as the undead. Their baggage, called "caskets," strengthened the association with the supernatural. The third Ursuline Convent, dating to 1751, which is claimed to be the oldest building in the Mississippi River valley, is a magnificent three-story building; to this day, there is a line of boarded-up windows on the third floor. The nuns are said to have imprisoned these undead charges in their building, not only to keep them inside but also, perhaps, to protect these vampires from the ravages of the sun.

The Originals weaves this legend of female vampires into the story of the Mikaelson family, who used to rule over the French Quarter, where the Ursuline Convent is located. Rebekah the sister vampire emerges as a heroine who rescues the Casket Girls from their intended fate as brides to brutish men. She thus claims New Orleans as her town, using the phrase "us girls have got to stick together" in the episode "The Casket Girls," which she will repeat over the centuries, often to females who are not supernaturals.

Many episodes open with a place and year. The first episode, "Always and Forever," opens with "Mississippi River, 300 years ago," and Elijah provides the voiceover. "The Casket Girls" begins "Louisiana Territory 1751," which is the date of construction of the third Ursuline Convent; Rebekah is the narrator, explaining, "For centuries people have been coming to New Orleans hoping for a fresh start, hoping to find fortune, adventure, even love . . . like the legendary Casket Girls." Rebekah characterizes the immigrants as "young society women imported from France with the promise of marrying a proper New Orleans gentleman." Instead of the nuns of legend, it is Rebekah the vampire who meets the young women with carriages; she travels with them to the city of New Orleans (the casket girls supposedly landed in what is now Mobile). As the camera pans the countryside, we see a gang of men bearing torches, blocking the road, and shouting, "We want to see the women!" As Rebekah wryly explains, "Little did they know that the men who awaited them were far from proper and not at all gentlemen." Extreme close-ups of the terrified young women's faces show their alarm, but then suddenly there are screams, followed by silence. As their male escort looks out the carriage door, he is abruptly pulled from the carriage and killed. A prim and proper Rebekah wipes her bloody lips, and reassures the women: "There, there little lambs. All the bad men have gone away." And then she informs them, "You're safe here. Please forgive all the disorder. Us girls have got to stick together." The young women flee with her, presumably to become the Casket Girl vampires. In this fashion, Rebekah reclaims New Orleans, a feminine city, for female supernaturals.

The series' episodes frequently jump from historical moments to present-day New Orleans. "The Casket Girls" begins with the origins of the legends and moves to a contemporary, wholly fictious Casket Girls Festival, in which the supernaturals wholeheartedly participate. The festival reinforces the idea that New Orleans is a vampire city and draws on the device of "vampires playing people playing vampires" that is also a feature of *Interview with the*

Vampire. In contemporary tourist New Orleans, the entire French Quarter is the stage. The camera pans the streets, showing throngs of costumed revelers, dancers, an old-fashioned carriage hearse drawn by a horse, vendors, musicians, and dancers. Drawing on elements of downtown Mardi Gras street parades, the scene includes large circular streamers brandished by marchers. Threading through the crowd are the vampires, who, despite the frivolity around them, are engaged in a deadly struggle for control of the French Quarter. Rebekah comments, "The Casket Girls legend lives on—now celebrated in typical New Orleans fashion with stylish costumes and supernatural flare. It's a yearly reminder of how women can be oppressed by selfish men and how they can triumph if brave enough to fight for themselves." Rebekah's comments apply not only to herself, as a female vampire oppressed and controlled by her brother Klaus, but also to Cami, a female psychologist/barmaid who is painfully having her memories—which were erased by Klaus—restored by a witch. Rebekah identifies the relevance of the Casket Girls legend when she proclaims, "This festival might as well be in my honor"—not only because she rescued the original Casket Girls but also because she is still fighting to protect women and herself from the male vampires who have taken advantage of her. Rebekah describes Davina, a witch treated badly by her brothers, as "a modern-day Casket Girl, used by witches, lied to by Marcel, manipulated by Elijah, threatened by Klaus." The female werewolf Hayley interrupts her, asking, "Are you talking about Davina or yourself?"

The scene then portrays more of the festival mayhem, which reflects the disorder in the supernatural community. Hayley dons a wedding dress as a costume, and a female-dominated troupe of skeleton-painted drummers lead a mass of people in the street. Women dressed as Casket Girls wear white wedding gowns, but their faces are dripping with blood, alluding to their vampirism. Female vampires, these marches remind viewers, can be as deadly as the male versions. A later scene takes place in a French Quarter courtyard of a mansion that used to be the Mikaelsons' home;

there Rebekah stabs Marcel with a dagger, telling him, "I trusted you, but you just used me to stay in power." Davina, who had been the hidden power behind vampire king Marcel's control of the French Quarter, threatens Rebekah, who cautions her about the male vampires. "Hunting people is such a boyish thing to do," she says. Exposing Marcel's cruelty, Rebekah shows Davina his crypt, where he tortures and leaves entombed vampires who have displeased him. She warns Davina and Cami, "Both of you have been lied to and taken advantage of by Marcel."

The human female Cami embodies Rebekah's feminist message and actions. Cami visits her uncle, a priest, confronting him about his collusion with evil supernaturals in the city. An enormous statue of Jesus in the back courtyard of St. Louis Cathedral is brightly illuminated during their visit. Her uncle has betrayed and lied to Cami, covering up the circumstances of her brother Sean's death at the hand of vampires. "You are every bit as bad as the other monsters in this city," Cami tells him. Through exposure of the church's collusion, *The Originals* suggests that human evil is as awful as any committed by the vampires. The church and the male vampires both run the city ruthlessly, and Rebekah and the other female characters, both human and supernatural, have had enough of their rule.

"The Casket Girls" continues as Rebekah rescues a collapsed Davina, picking her up and carrying her to the French Quarter mansion. As she does so, her voiceover explains, "It is said that this is a man's world and sometimes it is. For every Casket Girl that was saved, countless other were not. But women are far more resilient than they are given credit for." Echoing Rebekah's later lament that "I too am resilient, and I am tired of being oppressed," a strengthened Cami boldly walks up to Klaus and threatens to expose him as a vampire. As Rebekah rescues a male vampire entombed by Marcel in the crypt, feeding him blood from a hospital bag, she declares she is going to "take New Orleans right out from under all of their noses." Throughout the series Rebekah challenges and tries to ameliorate the cruelty of Marcel's and, later, her brother Klaus's cruel reigns. At the end of the series, she chooses freedom rather than ruling the French Quarter as its queen.

In later episodes of *The Originals,* the vampires defeat Papa Tunny, a Voodoo practitioner who uses sacrificial magic. The series portrays male-dominated Voodoo practitioners as even more abusive and destructive than vampires, who are rarely shown feeding. Rebekah may have a few spots of blood on her lips, but she daintily wipes them away with a handkerchief. Elijah and Klaus engage in bloody battles, even with deadly daggers, but they are not shown stalking human victims or draining them of blood, as graphically depicted in both the novel and film of *Interview with the Vampire.* As a result, the viewer can almost forget that the Mikaelson siblings must regularly drink blood from a human body to survive. Vampirism is shown as more of a lifestyle than as monstrous. *The Originals* thus expands Rice's one sympathetic vampire to create a family, who with their quarrels and affection for each other, resemble a human family. That they are rooted to New Orleans as their family home, despite their age of a thousand years, suggests the city's power as a place of vampires.

George R. R. Martin, well known as the writer of *Game of Thrones,* a series of novels and a television show about bloodthirsty humans, also wrote a vampire novel. *Fevre Dream,* published in 1982, a few years after *Interview with the Vampire,* similarly presents a struggle between old and new vampires, and again, the major site of struggle is New Orleans. Immigrants to the New World, these vampires reflect the very American notion that a jaded, decaying Old World needs to be revived by the new blood offered by the New World, especially that of New Orleans. The heroic Joshua York—a vampire who, like Louis, resists taking human life—is engaged in a struggle with Damon Julian, a much older vampire who is cruel and capricious like Lestat. Martin's human protagonist, Abner Marsh, who is a steamboat captain, becomes caught up in these struggles, which include the attempt by York to create a band of vampires who, like himself, will renounce killing humans and survive on an alternative blood drink. This novel is set just before the outbreak of the Civil War, making explicit parallels to brother fighting brother over the issue of slavery. Marsh remains unaware of vampirism at first, and his eventual commitment to York's cause suggests an optimistic view of vampire–human relations: the two species need not be trapped in the roles of predator and prey.

As with Rice's novel and its adaptations, the struggles between vampire leaders and humans remain a conflict of masculinities in *Fevre Dream*, although there are female vampires and they have moments of heroism. The city of New Orleans remains a feminine lure for male vampires and humans, often leading to their deaths. Making the character of Marsh a steamboat captain allows Martin to add in the spell of the Mississippi River and of the feminine ships as sites that the vampires struggle to dominate. Not only are ships traditionally referred to as "she/her" but their womblike qualities—carrying humans and cargo inside them—strengthen their feminine aspect. In the nineteenth century, steamboats were the conveyers of goods up the birth channel of rivers. Like the ships captained by men, the river—feminine because it is an aspect of Mother Nature—is a site of struggle for male figures who need to control it. During the Civil War, the river and modern shipping technology would be needed to maintain dominance and to ensure mobility of the competing forces.

Set in the mid-nineteenth century, *Fevre Dream* shows vampire leaders as representing both new and old models of male leadership. York has invented an alternative to killing humans, using chemistry, while Julian prefers to kill in the shadows, taking pleasure in tormenting his victims and then moving away when he exhausts humans' resources, both of blood and wealth. York socializes with humans, having renounced killing them, and hopes to convert other vampires to a peaceful coexistence with humans. Julian is a vicious autocrat, decadent and cruel, who treats other vampires capriciously, always threatening them with death and maintaining his control over them through violence.

Hundreds of years younger than Julian, York is a Byronic hero who actually knew Byron. He spends hours reading at night, quotes the poet Percy Bysshe Shelley and other Romantics, and writes in his journal. His cabin is filled with books. These activities reflect the evolution of the vampire. York has researched his people's history and realizes that as a species, the people of the night, as they call themselves, "have no language. We use human language, human names" (154). York's immersion in literature and history marks him as a civilized being. Julian, by contrast, sits in the dark in a mansion's library, surrounded by books "covered with dust . . . None of them had been touched in years. Damon Julian was not a reader" (19).

Both, however, are drawn to New Orleans for the safety that it offers them. Researching historical records, York has discovered a ship of vampires that headed for New Orleans, and he follows the trail of these vampires to the city (178). Julian has retreated to a plantation where he has mesmerized and then killed the human family. As the plantation's patriarch, he is a failure, allowing the building and land to rot and decay. One of the younger vampires, Karl, complains, "Dust everywhere, the house rotting, rats" (107). Like a beast, Julian will reside in the plantation until it falls apart and then move on to exterminate another wealthy family and live in their home. York, by contrast, has an appreciation for human structures and creations, and he bonds with Marsh by offering the steamboat captain the opportunity to build a beautiful steamboat named the *Fevre Dream,* which will be the fastest on the river. Although York is more polished, a gentleman, and a vampire with a soul, he is not as strong as the brutish Julian. But with the help of humans and Julian's abused vampire minions, York eventually defeats Julian. Like Rice, then, Martin valorizes New World vampires and, by implication, their chosen home as a place where justice can eventually prevail and a divided country can be reconciled.

While Rice's *Interview* exposed the racism that was used to justify the enslavement of people, Martin brings it to the foreground in his novel. Slavery is an original sin of humans, a parallel to the sin of vampires. Vampires have an alternative to draining humans of their blood and killing them, and so do the white enslavers who exploit the enslaved to generate huge profits from human misery. York confronts Marsh with the sins of slavery, explaining that while vampires are reviled by humans, "Here in New Orleans I have witnessed the way you enslave your own kind, whip them and sell them like animals" (175). Marsh is aware of the evils of enslavement, telling York that "I never held much with slavery. You can't just go . . . usin' another kind of people, as if they weren't people at all" (201). Marsh refuses to convey enslaved people as cargo, even though he would profit from it. He recruits Toby, an enslaved man he freed, to fight alongside York in this battle. Marsh realizes that New Orleans, as alluring and full of pleasures as it is, has a sickness at its core, as does the red fever that overtakes vampires and causes them to feed maniacally on human beings: "As he looked out over New Orleans, [Marsh muttered to himself] 'There's something rotten here'" (198).

York agrees. "The city is lovely . . . I have nothing but admiration for the Vieux Carré . . . This city—the heat, the bright colors, the smells, the slaves—it is very alive, this New Orleans, but inside I think it is rotten with sickness. Everything is so rich and beautiful here, the cuisine, the manners, the architecture, but beneath that . . ." (132). The core of the malaise is enslavement—the cruel exploitation that generates the wealth that makes possible New Orleans's external beauty. York understands this contrast between the beauty and its source: "You wander through the St. Louis and cast your eyes upon all the marble and that delightful dome with the light pouring through it down upon the rotunda, and then you learn it is a famous slave mart where humans are sold like cattle" (132–133). The people of the night traditionally used the term "cattle" for humans, but of the current vampires, only evil bloodmaster Julian does. York's use of the word makes explicit that the Old World vampire's predations are akin to those of slavery. York makes clear the choices that humans and vampires must make: "Our races [vampire and human] are not so very different. All of us have good and evil in us, and all of us dream" (322). Vampires, then, offer New Orleans, with its history of corruption and exploitation, a model of choosing not to be evil. If a Voodoo queen can use potions and evocations to bring justice, and ghosts can warn of injustice, vampires may move among humans to show us our own misdeeds, both historical and current. As York's love and frequent citation of literature show, art offers a way to explore and expose human frailty. That vampires are drawn to New Orleans suggests that its stories and legends offer the same mirror to the United States' original sins and failings.

Why then are vampires so glamorized and sought after? As a deluded rich matron jumps during the Théâtre des Vampires to offer herself to the evil vampire Armand, she shouts, "Take me, monsieur! I adore you!" (*Interview with the Vampire,* film). Why do humans adore vampires, and relatedly, why do they love New Orleans? The common features of vampire texts, novels, films, non-fiction books, and walking tours suggest that it is the frisson of recognition—the desire for power and allure shared by vampires and humans—or, as Nina Auerbach proclaims in her book title, "our vampires [are] ourselves," that is the source of this love.

CONCLUSION

X X X

New Orleans's storied record of supernatural happenings shows that it well deserves the title of America's "most haunted city." The dark enchantment of the city's beautiful eighteenth- and nineteenth-century buildings, its bordering the Mississippi River, its terrible association with enslavement, and its rich fusion of cultures attract millions of visitors every year. Although *City of the Undead* focuses on Voodoo practitioners, ghosts, and vampires, there are undoubtedly other books to be written on witches, werewolves, and other paranormal beings. And this book has by no means exhausted all that can be written about Voodoo, ghosts, and vampires.

A thread that connects these three classes of supernatural creatures is the special appeal of the city for their kind. Supernatural beings seem to be more comfortable in places such as the French Quarter, where walking is the dominant mode of travel and mule-drawn carriages still traverse the streets. Voodoo practitioners, ghosts, and vampires seem to belong in port cities like New Orleans, where for centuries, people from many countries have come and gone and where travelers throng the streets. This context allows the undead to blend in more easily with the living. The city's tradition of costuming—especially during Carnival season but seen throughout the year—also encourages anonymity and unusual behaviors. And perhaps most importantly, New Orleans has long been known for its tolerance, even encouragement, of licentious activities prohibited elsewhere. Storyville, the legalized area of prostitution, only existed from 1897 to 1917, but the attitude that created the district predated and followed its legal extinction. Artists and writers like Tennessee Williams and William Faulkner, among others, were drawn to the French Quarter for its beauty and its bohemian acceptance (and inexpensive rents). That New Orleans has historically been more accepting of LBGTQ+ individuals and has had the largest numbers of Black homeowners in the United States are other signs of its relative inclusivity. The numerous free people of color who had and continue to have a strong impact on the city are another unique feature—Marie Laveau's relative freedom was made possible by the French Code Noir, in effect nowhere else in the United States. The fusion of Native American, African, and Caribbean beliefs and practices also encouraged a complex and hybrid spirituality. Other cities may have some of these features, but none has their intense combination that is so fruitful for supernatural events and narratives.

And of course, New Orleans has embraced its supernatural reputation. Its tourist bureau encourages conventions and visitors who focus on the paranormal. Real estate brokers advertise homes as "haunted" or "not haunted." The city's walking tours attract thousands of tourists, with hundreds swarming the French Quarter and cemeteries every day. Writers and television and film showrunners have made the city one of the busiest of production centers. The state's generous tax benefits are partly responsible for the scale of film and TV production, but examining the types of shows produced in New Orleans reveals a heavy emphasis on supernatural content, from *American Horror Story* to *The Originals.* Even medical detective television dramas like *Bones* show the impact of New Orleans's supernatural history, with skeptical doctors and cops encountering the paranormal in the city.

New Orleans's supernatural side enables the paranormal to fulfill an important need: to encourage the living to confront their demons, the undead. In a society that prefers death and dying to take place offstage, out of sight, belief in the supernatural encourages consideration of mortality. It offers hope that there is an afterlife, but at the same time teaches the lesson that an undead existence may come with a high price. Immortality, as seen in representations of Voodoo, ghosts, and vampires, suggests that the living should cherish their status and accept death when it comes.

The supernatural contains within it the repressed: not just fear of death but also the innumerable cultural repressions and forgettings—the elisions of history too horrible to be preserved. Voodoo queens, ghosts, and vampires, in this view, represent the living people excised from power and even dignity. Supernatural beings thus function as stand-ins for the "othered," such as LBGTQ+ people, people of color, Native Americans, and women. In a process of defamiliarization, paranormal beings represent living people. Supernatural literature, film, television, and walking tours remind us why we fear the paranormal. It represents a challenge to life as we know it—just as women offer a challenge to patriarchy, LBGTQ+ people contradict assumptions of heteronormativity, and people of color show there are alternatives to white supremacy and capitalism. For example, even though tour guides may want to reclaim Marie Laveau as an "entrepreneur," the Voodoo queen and her followers threatened the very basis on which enslavement was based. That threat is one reason Voodoo was made illegal. The supernatural represents alternatives to what seems a settled world of the living.

A final useful function of these supernatural creatures is that they allow visitors, readers, and viewers to confront injustice in its many forms—from racism and enslavement, sexism and misogyny, to wars, pestilence, and plague—and to acknowledge the sufferings that people endured in the past. The paranormal gives voice to the voiceless, those excluded from history. In the stories of victims of injustice who persist past their death, undead beings function as a conscience. What we do with this knowledge rests with the living. At worst, the undead can function as a cathartic release. Yes, evil and violence happened, and we can recognize it in New Orleans. But then visitors can return to their own cities and towns and bracket the experience off, turn it into a travel tale. At best, we can internalize the narrative and vow that future supernatural stories will not expose our complicity in the injustices of our time.

WORKS CITED

x x x

Abrahams, Roger D., with Nick Spitzer, John F. Szwed, and Robert Faris Thompson. 2006. *Blues for New Orleans*. Philadelphia: University of Pennsylvania Press.

Ambrose, Kala. 2012. *Spirits of New Orleans: Voodoo Curses, Vampire Legends, and Cities of the Dead*. Covington, KY: Clerisy Press.

Andrew, Jeffrey. 2010. "Vampires, Vampires, Everywhere!" *Phi Kappa Phi Forum* 90, no. 3 (Fall): 4–5.

Andrew, Scott. 2002. "Inside the World of Real-Life Vampires in New Orleans and Atlanta." October 29, 2022. https://www.cnn.com/2022/10/29/us /real-vampires-new-orleans-atlanta-cec.

Angelou, Maya. (1969) 2009. *I Know Why the Caged Bird Sings*. New York: Random House.

Antonijevic, Predrag, dir. 2011. *Ghost of New Orleans*. Hollywood: Little Murder Productions.

Auerbach, Nina. 1995. *Our Vampires, Ourselves*. Chicago: University of Chicago Press.

Belenky, Mary Field, Blythe McVicker Clinchy, Nancy Rule Goldberger, and Jill Matrick Tarule. 1986. *Women's Ways of Knowing: The Development of Self, Voice, and Mind*. New York: Basic Books.

Blayde, Ariadne. 2022. *Ash Tuesday*. Self-published.

Brooks, James, prod. 2018. *The Simpsons*. Episode, "Lisa Gets the Blues." Aired on April 22, 2018, on Fox.

Brown, Alan. 2020. *The Haunted South*. Charleston: Haunted America/History Press.

Browning, John Edgar. 2015. "The Real Vampires of New Orleans and Buffalo: A Research Note towards Comparative Ethnography." *Palgrave Communications*. doi: 10.1057/palcomms.2015.6 1–8.

Caskey, James. 2013. *The Haunted History of New Orleans: Ghosts of the French Quarter.* Savannah: Manta Ray Books.

Castranovo, Russ. 2001. *Necro Citizenship: Death, Eroticism, and the Public Sphere in the Nineteenth-Century United States.* Durham, NC: Duke University Press.

Chiorazzi, Anthony. 2015. "The Spirituality of Africa." [Interview with Jacob Olupona]. https://news.harvard.edu/gazette/story/2015/10/the-spirituality-of-africa/.

Clark, Emily Suzanne. 2020. "Nineteenth-Century New Orleans Voudou: An American Religion." *American Religion* 2, no. 1: 131–155.

Crandle, Marita Woywod. 2017. *New Orleans Vampires: History and Legend.* Charleston: History Press.

David, Alan, and Ron Kratz, prod. *Ghost Hunters.* Episode, "French Quarter Phantoms." Aired on March 16, 2011, on SyFy.

Day, William Patrick. 2002. *Vampire Legends in Contemporary American Culture: What Becomes a Legend Most.* Lexington: University Press of Kentucky.

de Caro, Frank. 2015. "*Ghost Stories of Old New Orleans* as a Source and a Model." *Louisiana Folklore Miscellany* 25: 1–7.

Dedek, Peter B. 2017. *The Cemeteries of New Orleans: A Cultural History.* Baton Rouge: LSU Press.

deLavigne, Jeanne. (1946) 2013. *Ghosts of Old New Orleans,* edited by Frank de Caro. Baton Rouge: LSU Press.

Dier, Brett. "50+ Beautiful Ghost Quotes from across Literature and Culture." Accessed July 8, 2022. https://kidadl.com/quotes/beautiful-ghost-quotes-from-across-literature-and-culture.

Eaton, Alexandra, Christoph Koettl, Quincy J. Ledbetter, Victoria Simpson, and Aaron Byrd. 2021. "Searching for the Lost Graves of Louisiana's Enslaved People." *New York Times,* June 27, 2021 (video).

Fandrich, Ina J. 2007 "Yorùbá Influences on Haitian Vodou and New Orleans Voodoo." *Journal of Black Studies* 37 (2007): 775–791.

Fensterstock, Allison. 2009. "Apertifs and Apparitions." *Times-Picayune,* October 30, 2009.

Garrison, Tim Alan, and Greg O'Brien, eds. 2017. *The Native South: New Histories and Enduring Legacies.* Lincoln: University of Nebraska. http://ebookcentral.proquest.com/lib/uark-ebooks/detail.action?docID=4865009.

Gehman, Mary, and Nancy Ries. (1988) 2013. *Women and New Orleans.* Donaldsville, LA: Margaret Media.

Gordon, Avery. (1997) 2008. *Ghostly Matters: Haunting and the Sociological Imagination*. Minneapolis: University of Minnesota Press.

Green, Tara T. 2012. "Voodoo Feminism through the Lens of Jewell Parker Rhodes' *Voodoo Dreams*." *Women's Studies* 41, no. 3: 282–302.

Harris, LaShawn. 2016. *Sex Workers, Psychics, and Numbers Runners: Black Women in New York City's Underground Economy*. Urbana: University of Illinois Press.

Hemard, Ned. 2011. "New Orleans Nostalgia: Is New Orleans Feminine?" Presentation to the New Orleans Bar Association, 2011.

Heyrman, Christine Leigh. 2000. "Native American Religion in Early America." *Divining America,* TeacherServe. Washington, DC: National Humanities Center. http://nationalhumanitiescenter.org/tserve/eighteen/ekeyinfo/natrel.html.

Hill, Erin, 2013. "Oh, Holy Night: Christmas with John Waters." *Antigravity* 113 (December): 21–22.

Jacobs, Claude F. 2001. "'Folk' for Whom? Tourist Guidebooks, Local Color, and the Spiritual Churches of New Orleans." *Journal of American Folklore* 114, no. 453: 309–330.

Jacobs, Claude Francis, and Andrew Kaslow. 1991. *The Spiritual Churches of New Orleans: Origins, Beliefs, and Rituals of an African-American Religion*. Knoxville: University of Tennessee Press.

Jeffries, Karen. 2022. Personal interview conducted by author, November 11, 2002, in New Orleans.

Johnson, Mark, and Rolin Jones. Prod. *Interview with the Vampire*. Episode "In the Throes of Increasing Wonder." Aired on October 2, 2022, on AMC.

Johnson, Rheta Grimley. 2019. "Voodoofest on Rue Dumaine and the Spirited Woman behind It." http://www.frenchquarterjournal.com.

Johnson, Walter. 1999. *Soul by Soul: Life inside the Antebellum Slave Market*. Cambridge, MA: Harvard University Press.

Jordan, Neil, dir. 1994. *Interview with the Vampire*. Hollywood: Warner Bros.

King, Grace. 1915. *New Orleans: The Place and the People*. New York: Macmillan.

Kissell, Joe. 2021. "New Orleans Cemeteries: Cities of the Dead." Interesting Thing of the Day, July 7, 2021. https://itotd.com/articles/6809/new-orleans-cemeteries.

Krist, Gary. 2015. *Empire of Sin: A Story of Sex, Jazz, Murder, and the Battle for Modern New Orleans*. New York: Crown.

Long, Carolyn Morrow. 2006. *A New Orleans Voudou Priestess: The Legend and Reality of Marie Laveau*. Gainesville: University Press of Florida.

———. 2012. *Madame Lalaurie: Mistress of the Haunted House.* Gainesville: University Press of Florida.

"Louisiana Outpaces Los Angeles, New York and All Others in 2013 Film Production, Study Shows." 2014. https://www.nola.com/entertainment_life/movies_tv/article_f088ed8d-95f3-5739-b2ed-e6c9a6be1865.html.

Lussier, Patrick, dir. 2000. *Dracula 2000.* Hollywood: Dimension Films.

Macdonald, Kirsty A. 2012. "Writing the Supernatural." In *The Edinburgh Companion to Scottish Women's Writing,* edited by Glenda Norquay, 94–102. Edinburgh: Edinburgh University Press.

Martin, George R. R. 1982. *Fevre Dream.* New York: Bantam.

Martin, Kameelah L. 2016. *Envisioning Black Feminist Voodoo Aesthetics: African Spirituality in American Cinema.* https://ebookcentral.proquest.com/lib/uark-ebooks/detail.action?docID=4659712.

Mellor, Louisa. 2018. "Top 50 TV Witches." *Den of Geek,* October 26, 2018. https://www.proquest.com/docview/2125480710?accountid=8361&pq-origsite=summon

Midlo Hall, Gwendolyn. 1992. *Africans in Colonial Louisiana: The Development of Afro-Creole Culture in the Eighteenth Century.* Baton Rouge: LSU Press.

Miles, Tiya. 2015. *Tales from the Haunted South: Dark Tourism and Memories of Slavery from the Civil War Era.* Chapel Hill: University of North Carolina Press.

Moers, Ellen. (1976) 1985. *Literary Women.* Oxford: Oxford University Press.

Moody, Donna L. 2014. "Intersecting Symbols in Indigenous American and African Material Culture: Diffusion or Independent Invention and Who Decides?" Master's thesis, February 2014. https://scholarworks.umass.edu/cgi/viewcontent.cgi?article=2152&context=theses.

Murphy, Ryan, and Brad Falchuk, prod. 2013–2014. *American Horror Story: Coven.* Aired on FX.

Murphy, Ryan, and Brad Falchuk, prod. 2013–2014. Episode, "Boy Parts." *American Horror Story.* Aired October 16, 2013, on FX.

Murphy, Ryan, and Brad Falchuk, prod. 2013–2014. Episode, "Fearful Pranks Ensue." *American Horror Story.* Aired October 30, 2013, on FX.

"New Orleans Film Industry Expected to Exceed $1 Billion in 2022." April 21, 2002. https://www.fox8live.com/2022/04/21/new-orleans-film-industry-expected-exceed-1-billion-2022.

"New Orleans' LaLaurie House Has Gruesome Past." 2013. https://www.forbes.com/sites/zillow/2013/10/23/new-orleans-lalaurie-house-has-gruesome-past/?sh=321b1ec2df48.

O'Reilly, Jennifer. 2019. "'We're More Than Just Pins and Dolls and Seeing the Future in Chicken Parts': Race, Magic and Religion in *American Horror Story: Coven*." *European Journal of American Culture* 38, no. 1: 29–41.

Osbey, Brenda Marie. 2011. "Why We Can't Talk to You about Voodoo." *Southern Literary Journal* 43 (Spring): 1–11.

Osborn, Royce, dir. 2003. *All on a Mardi Gras Day*. Aired on Public Broadcasting System.

Patterson, Orlando. 1982. *Slavery and Social Death*. Cambridge, MA: Harvard University Press.

Piatti-Farnell, Lorna. 2017. "'The Blood Never Stops Flowing and the Party Never Ends': *The Originals* and the Afterlife of New Orleans as a Vampire City." *M/C Journal* 20, no. 5. doi:10.5204/mcj.1314.

Pile, Steve. 2005. *Real Cities: Modernity, Space, and the Phantasmagorias of City Life*. Thousand Oaks, CA: Sage.

Plec, Julie, dir. 2013. *The Originals*. Episode, "The Casket Girls." Aired on October 3, 2013, on CW.

Plec, Julie, dir. 2013. *The Originals*. Episode, "Forever and Always." Aired on January 14, 2014, on CW.

Pulliam, June. 2014. *Monstrous Bodies: Feminine Power in Young Adult Horror Fiction*. Jefferson, NC: McFarland.

Quashie, Kevin E. 1997. "Mining Magic, Mining Dreams: A Conversation with Jewell Parker Rhodes." *Callaloo* 20, no. 2 (Spring): 431–440.

Rhodes, Jewell Parker. 1993. *Voodoo Dreams: A Novel of Marie Laveau*. New York: Picador.

Rice, Anne. 1976. *Interview with the Vampire*. New York: Ballantine.

Rice, Anne, and Christopher Rice, prod. 2022. *Interview with the Vampire*. Episode, "In the Throes of Increasing Wonder." Aired on October 7, 2022, on AMC.

Richard, C. E. 2003. *Louisiana: An Illustrated History*. Aired on Louisiana Public Broadcasting.

Roach, Joseph. 1996. *Cities of the Dead: Circum-Atlantic Performance*. New York: Columbia University Press.

Roberts, Kodi. 2015. *Voodoo and Power: The Politics of Religion in New Orleans, 1881–1940*. Baton Rouge: LSU Press.

Roberts, Robin. 2019. *Subversive Spirits: The Female Ghost in British and American Popular Culture*. Jackson: University Press of Mississippi.

Roberts, Robin. 2019. "Sustaining Culture: Dianne Honoré, History, and Parading Traditions in New Orleans: A Conversation." *Journal of American Culture* 42, no. 1 (March): 49–54.

Rose, Chris. 2009. "Comfortable in Our Own Skin: Antoinette K-Doe's Funeral Proved Why We Live and Die in New Orleans." *Times-Picayune,* March 9, 2009.

Rout, Kathleen. 2003. "Who Do You Love? Anne Rice's Vampires and Their Moral Transition." *Journal of Popular Culture* 36, no. 3 (Winter): 473–479.

Schwab, Victoria. 2021. *Bridge of Souls.* New York: Scholastic.

Smith, Kalila Katherine. 1998. *Journey into Darkness: Ghosts and Vampires of New Orleans.* New Orleans: De Simonin Publications.

Solnit, Rebecca, and Rebecca Snedeker. 2013. *Unfathomable City: A New Orleans Atlas.* Berkeley: University of California Press.

Spera, Keith. 2011. *Groove Interrupted: Loss, Renewal, and the Music of New Orleans.* New York: St. Martin's Press.

Stanonis, Anthony J. 2012. "Dead but Delightful: Tourism and Memory in New Orleans Cemeteries." In *Destination Dixie: Tourism and Southern History,* edited by Karen L. Cox. Gainesville: University Press of Florida.

Starr, S. Frederick. 1985. "New Orleans." *Wilson Quarterly* 9 (1985): 156–169.

Sublette, Ned. 2008. *The World That Made New Orleans: From Spanish Silver to Congo Square.* Chicago: Lawrence Hill.

Tallant, Robert. (1945) 1988. *Gumbo Ya-Ya: Folktales of Louisiana.* Gretna, LA: Pelican.

———. (1946) 2003. *Voodoo in New Orleans.* Gretna, LA. Pelican.

———. (1956) 1984. *The Voodoo Queen.* Mt. Pleasant, SC: Arcadia Press.

Taylor, Troy. 2010. *Wicked New Orleans: The Dark Side of the Big Easy.* Charleston: History Press.

Tolliver, Domonique. 2021. "Ancestors, Pray for Us." *Gambit,* July 14, 2021. https://www.nola.com/gambit/news/article_05c27d66-e4cd-11eb-bc2e-a3a97e5a93cf.html.

Wade, Leslie, Robin Roberts, and Frank de Caro. 2019. *Downtown Mardi Gras: New Carnival Practices in Post-Katrina New Orleans.* Jackson: University Press of Mississippi.

Wall, Bennett, John Rodrigue, and Light T. Cummins. 2014. *Louisiana: A History.* 6th ed. Chichester, UK: John Wiley.

Ward, Martha. 2004. *Voodoo Queen: The Spirited Lives of Marie Laveau.* Jackson: University Press of Mississippi.

Webster, Richard A. 2009. "New Orleans City Business." *City Business,* October 7, 2009.

Wehmeyer, Stephen C. 2007. "'Indians at the Door': Power and Placement on New Orleans Spiritual Church Altars." *Western Folklore* 66: 1/2 (Winter/Spring): 15–44.

Weinstock, Jeffrey. 2008. *Scare Tactics: Supernatural Fiction by American Women*. New York: Fordham University Press.

Wilkins, Amy C. 2008. *Wannabees, Goths, and Christians: The Boundaries of Sex, Style, and Status*. Chicago: University of Chicago Press.

Wilson, Hugh, prod. *Frank's Place*. Pilot episode, "Frank's Return." Aired on September 14, 1987, on CBS.

———. *Frank's Place*. Episode, "Frank Returns." Aired on September 21, 1987, on CBS.

———. *Frank's Place*. Episode, "Frank Takes Charge." Aired on September 28, 1987, on CBS.

———. *Frank's Place*. Episode, "Disengaged." Aired on October 26, 1987, on CBS.

———. *Frank's Place*. Episode, "Dueling Voodoo." Aired on January 11, 1988, on CBS.

Witucki, Ann. 2022. Personal interview conducted by author, November 12, 2022, in New Orleans.

Woods, W. S. 1951. "L'Abbé Prévost and the Gender of New Orleans." *Modern Language Notes* 66 (April): 259–261.

INDEX

X X X

vampires, 1–2, 4–5, 7–10, 12–13, 27, 41–47, *48*, 53, 81, 91, 97, 108, 121, 125–66, *156*, 167, 169; female, 45, 128, 137, 142, 150–52, 158, 160, 163; identity, 131

Vieux Carré Commission, 120

violence, 23, 39, 42, 91–93, 103, 131–32, 138, 155, 163, 169

Vlad Tepes, 125

Vlad the Impaler (Vlad Dracula), 132

Voodoo, 1–5, 7, 9, 15, 19–21, 28–37, 47, 49–53, 57, 59–86, *80*, *81*, 91–93, 95, 97, 104, 107–9, 124, 127–29, 135–36, 147, 152, 161–62, 167, 169; African Vodun, 14, 28; Haitian Vodou, 14, 28, 34, 35, 52; queens and priestesses, 5, 8, 10, 12–13, 34, 39, 47, *48*, 50, *51*, 52–53, 57, *65*, 77, 79–81, 91–93, 128, 138, 166; shops, 7, 35, 37, 49–50, 77, *80*, *81*, *82*, 84

Voodoo and Power (Roberts), 49, 66

Voodoo Authentica, 30, 50–51, 84

Voodoo Dreams (Rhodes), 7, 36, 50, 55, 69, 71–73, 86

Voodoo feminism, 36, 50, 68–86

Voodoofest, 50–51, *51*

Voodoo in New Orleans (Tallant), 69

Voodoo Museum, *83*

Voodoo Queen, The (Tallant), 69

"Voodoo Song," 36

walking tours, 1, 3–4, 6, 8, 10, 11, 23, 29, 34, 37, 40–41, 43, 50, 73, 81, 83–86,

87, 89–91, 93, 95–97, 117–19, 121, 124, 138, 156, 158, 166, 168–69

Wall, Bennett, 24

Wall Street Journal, 54

Ward, Martha, 30–31, 68–69

Waters, John, 54

Wehmeyer, Stephen C., 16

Weinstock, Jeffrey, 7, 91

werewolves, 153–55, 158, 160, 167

white supremacy, 5, 29, 33–34, 37, 42, 55, 68–69, 72–73, 77–78, 91, 169

Wicked New Orleans, 43

Wilkins, Amy C., 129

Williams, Tennessee, 168

Williams, Willy, 36

witches and witchcraft, 61–62, 73–74, 76–81, 104–5, 138, 155, 160, 167

"Witch Queen of New Orleans," 36

Witucki, Ann, 51–52

women, 5, 8, 11, 13, 15, 19, 24, 29–31, 34–35, 37, 39, 42, 45–46, 50, 52–53, 55, 58–59, 61, 64, 68, 72, 81, 86, 90–93, 103, 118–22, 136–37, 148, 151, 160–61, 169; Black, 56–57, 69–74, 78, 83, 91, 100–101; Creole, 85; Scottish, 55; white, 52, 55, 72–74, 78, 83, 86, 100

Women in New Orleans (Gehman and Ries), 158

Woods, William S., 53

Works Progress Administration, 30, 33, 124

zombies, 1–3, 28, 31, 33, 34, 50, 75–76